Praise for *Outsmarting Social Media*

"Evan's understanding of marketing psychology is impressive. Through the lens of social media, he makes key observations about how people search for information and why."

—Richard Isaacson, Harvard-trained neurologist and associate professor of
  clinical neurology

"This book is eye-opening. It states, in simple terms, precisely how to dominate social media in your chosen field."

—Dr. Stephen Gullo, national bestselling author and former Columbia University
  professor

"This book provides crucial insights and practical solutions for anyone looking to use social media as a platform to grow their business or nonprofit. It's a must-read for anyone interested in seizing the immense opportunities made available by Facebook, Twitter, LinkedIn, and all social platforms."

—Darian Rodriguez Heyman, Editor, *Nonprofit Management 101: A Complete and
  Practical Guide for Leaders and Professionals*

"There are thousands of people running around calling themselves "social media experts." The very fact that Evan has never done that speaks volumes. Evan lets his work on behalf of major-name clients do the talking for him."

—Peter Shankman, founder of Help a Reporter Out, author, and marketing consultant

"If you have ever asked whether social media could help your your business reach potential customers, this book answers an enthusiastic "yes!" and then goes on to explain exactly how with imagination, ingenuity, and creativity. Evan Bailyn provides a detailed understanding of the fast-changing online world of social networks and draws fearless predictions as to where it's going and what it will mean to consumers and businesses."

—Anne Kennedy, International Search Strategist and author of *Global Search Engine
  Marketing*

"In Outsmarting Social Media, Evan Bailyn shines a laser beam on the new currency of the Internet. The new currency is friends helping friends decide what to do, buy, or try. Marketers, if you thought the Wild West was wild, this is wilder; saddle up and be prepared to ride at dawn."

—Roy Spence, Chairman of GSD&M and CEO of The Purpose I̶n̶t̶

D1218229

OUTSMARTING SOCIAL MEDIA

Profiting in the Age of Friendship Marketing

EVAN BAILYN

800 East 96th Street,
Indianapolis, Indiana 46240 USA

Outsmarting Social Media: Profiting in the Age of Friendship Marketing

ISBN-13: 978-0-7897-4939-0

ISBN-10: 0-7897-4939-4

Library of Congress Cataloging-in-Publication data is on file.

First Printing: March 2012

Trademarks

Warning and Disclaimer

Bulk Sales

Que Publishing offers excellent discounts on this book when ordered in quantity for bulk purchases or special sales. For more information, please contact

> U.S. Corporate and Government Sales
> 1-800-382-3419
> corpsales@pearsontechgroup.com

For sales outside of the U.S., please contact

> International Sales
> international@pearson.com

Editor-in-Chief
Greg Wiegand

Acquisitions Editor
Rick Kughen

Development Editor
Rick Kughen

Managing Editor
Sandra Schroeder

Project Editor
Seth Kerney

Copy Editor
Barbara Hacha

Indexer
Lisa Stumpf

Proofreader
Debbie Williams

Technical Editor
Mark Reddin

Publishing Coordinator
Cindy Teeters

Interior Designer
Anne Jones

Cover Designer
Anne Jones

Compositor
Mark Shirar

CONTENTS AT A GLANCE

TABLE OF CONTENTS

About the Author

Evan Bailyn is an Internet entrepreneur and author of *Outsmarting Google: SEO Secrets to Winning New Business* (Que Publishing, 2011, ISBN 9780789741035). Evan's web properties have been visited by more than 50 million people. After graduating from Columbia University in 2003, Evan taught himself about search engines, quickly discovering how to rank at the top of Google for any search term. He then established a network of education-related businesses, which he later sold.

In January 2006, he founded Cartoon Doll Emporium, one of the largest children's websites in the world. The company received an investment from Allen & Co. one year later, and by 2010, the company was sold.

Currently, Mr. Bailyn offers marketing services through his companies, First Page Sage and Good Media Co. Under his tutelage, clients have established the predominant websites in their industries, become *New York Times* bestselling authors, and grown multimillion dollar product lines. His voice can be found on the social media pages of celebrities worldwide.

Mr. Bailyn has been interviewed on ABC News and Fox News and featured in the *New York Times*, *The Wall Street Journal*, the *New York Post*, *Crain's*, *Forbes*, and *Advertising Age*.

Dedication

To my wife Sasha–You inspire me every day.

To my big brother Brad–I couldn't have asked for a more capable and supportive partner.

Acknowledgments

Peter Shankman–I will always be grateful to you for sparking my writing career.

Rick Kughen–Thank you for the opportunity to create this book, and for your encouragement and support.

Matt Gielen–Even gurus have teachers, and you are one of mine.

Ryan Gielen–Thanks for your knowledge, generosity, and trustworthiness.

Darian Rodriguez Heyman–You have been an incredible model for doing good.

Chris Robb–Thanks for consistently reminding me that there is a greater purpose for my work.

Hyla Molander–I am so grateful for your friendship and inspiration.

Russell, Mom, and Dad–I love you guys so much.

We Want to Hear from You!

As the reader of this book, *you* are our most important critic and commentator. We value your opinion and want to know what we're doing right, what we could do better, what areas you'd like to see us publish in, and any other words of wisdom you're willing to pass our way.

As an Editor-in-Chief for Que Publishing, I welcome your comments. You can email or write me directly to let me know what you did or didn't like about this book—as well as what we can do to make our books better.

Please note that I cannot help you with technical problems related to the topic of this book. We do have a User Services group, however, where I will forward specific technical questions related to the book.

When you write, please be sure to include this book's title and author as well as your name, email address, and phone number. I will carefully review your comments and share them with the author and editors who worked on the book.

Email: feedback@quepublishing.com

Mail: Greg Wiegand
            Editor-in-Chief
            Que Publishing
            800 East 96th Street
            Indianapolis, IN 46240 USA

Reader Services

Visit our website and register this book at informit.com/register for convenient access to any updates, downloads, or errata that might be available for this book.

Introduction

I am not an author by trade. I'm an entrepreneur. For that reason, this book does not contain any highfalutin academic theory or smart-sounding tech jargon. Instead, it contains real, effective strategies that have made me and my clients millions of dollars and can do the same for your business. Every word of this book is based on years of being in the trenches, analyzing the algorithms and executive decisions at companies like Google, Facebook, YouTube, and Twitter. If used properly, this book can propel a person to the same level of knowledge as someone who eats, breathes, and sleeps social media. A truly creative mind can turn the information in this book into worldwide recognition for their brand.

Most companies that I've worked with have come to me with the same issue: They don't understand how to use social media. Well, using social media is fairly easy. You just need to have a genuine message for the world and start interesting conversations with your fans or followers. A greater challenge is building an audience. These same businesses, who have had tremendous exposure in the press, have never communicated with their customers directly. After working with my company, they were able to find the hundreds of thousands of people who would have loved to speak with them but didn't know they could. And better yet, they connected with new customers who noticed the attention they were getting and wanted to learn more about them. That's the beauty of the social Internet.

A good marketer is always a kind of social engineer, a beater of systems. It doesn't matter what the system is, or whether it's online or offline; they will find a way to get the advantage. They *always* do things ethically, but never take a rule at face value. There are some people who like to do things the safe way—take your time, spend a lot of money, and follow the road that many before you have taken. If you're one of those people, this book may not be for you. But if you are a person who is fascinated by the sheer power of social media as a marketing tool and are looking to leverage it for all it is worth, you're in for a good ride.

Beating a search engine or social network begins with what I call the Wild West Principle: There is always a place somewhere that is rich in gold yet has grown too quickly for its own good. Therefore, its rules have not had time to be tested, and it is ripe for mining. Google between 2006 and 2009 was very much a Wild West for search engine optimizers. If you bought text-based links that pointed to your website, placing your keywords inside the text (for example: high heeled shoes), you could quickly reach the top of the search rankings. But by 2010, Google had fully blocked this technique, much to the chagrin of hundreds of companies who had used it to dominate the search listings. Even big businesses like JC Penney had been employing this strategy, and none were happy when Google ended the party.

But they should have expected it. That is how the Wild West works. There are booms and busts, and gold rush towns disappear overnight. The real question is: How much money did each company make before Google figured out how to turn the Wild West into a well-ordered society?

Some may be tempted to take advantage of a fledgling Wild West by scamming it. That's what hucksters have done to email over the years, setting up phishing schemes with fake stories about lottery wins and rich relatives in other countries. Unfortunately, many bright people have chosen to use their energy in this unethical manner. And sure, Wild Wests are wide open for them. But scamming—and in the context of the Internet, that means *spamming*—represents very short-term thinking. Spamming works for a little while and then gets you banned. Playing *within* the rules but stretching them a little bit is a far better course of action. The difference between the two is like the difference between holding up a saloon and starting a rival saloon next door that has better entertainment and stronger drinks. Both methods will make you money, but the latter will do far better for you in the long term, not to mention keep you out of trouble. In my opinion, it never makes sense to spam.

Social media, the subject of this book, is very much a Wild West. It probably will remain that way for the next few years, because it is so new and there is no concrete idea of how it will work yet. In the following chapters, I outline how you should be thinking about social media as it evolves, as well as the ways to use it to your economic advantage.

When writing this book, I was careful to create strategies that are likely to work not just today, but into the future. A lot of changes occur in the world of search and social media each month, but even more *doesn't* change. My theories and suggestions are based on this bedrock, the stuff that remains constant. Usually, that places my focus squarely on the things that drive revenue to companies like Google and Facebook. For example, we know that Facebook makes most of its money by serving small advertisements to its users. It is reasonable, then, to conclude that it will continue this program for a long time to come. That is why I have devoted a great deal of time, and a chapter of this book, to getting an advantage with Facebook ads. In contrast, it would not have made sense for me to meditate on Google Buzz, a social product that existed from 2010 to 2011, because Google never derived any real revenue from it.

Much of the information in this book may seem speculative to you, and that's because social media is still in its nascent phases. However, my theories are based on a deep analysis of the companies pioneering the social age, statements the companies have made about future plans, and exclusive interviews with their current and past employees. I feel very confident that this book addresses most of the new products we'll see in the coming time.

If you are a marketer and are wondering whether this is the right book to be reading, ask yourself whether Google, Facebook, Twitter, and YouTube are important to your business. If they are, know that socializing the Web, in some form or another, is the biggest initiative that each of these companies is working on right now. Gaining an understanding of social media in its early stages will give you a tremendous advantage as it evolves to define the next phase of the Internet.

Here's the thing: We have reached the age of infinite information. More interesting things are produced on the Internet in a single day than you could consume in your lifetime. That's a problem Google, Facebook, Microsoft, and hundreds of other companies have been dealing with for years. But it used to be the goal.

Getting to the point where all the information we could ever want was at our fingertips was the great challenge of the first phase of the Internet. The next great challenge was organizing that information. Many companies offered us solutions. Yahoo gave us the portal—one place where you could check the weather, read the headlines, book a vacation, and buy a car. Search engines broke new ground when they offered us a way of sorting through every web page out there with one click. Blogs gave us the day's best content according to a single curator. Wikipedia gave us a group-edited, constantly updated, completely searchable encyclopedia.

Then we entered the third phase of the Internet, a time when social information became the center of our world. Twitter popularized the status update—a short report on what you are doing right now. Facebook redefined our social lives by allowing us to check in with everyone we've ever known, and took it a step further by defining the people in our lives by their likes and interests. Now we are swimming in a sea of information, not just about stuff, but about *us*, our unique circle of friends, and we've got more than we know what to do with. A new challenge is thus born: how to make use of so much seemingly useless data. Who will come along and slurp up millions of reports on what people had for breakfast, watched on TV, and thought about the latest political controversy, and give it back to us in a format we care about?

Both Google and Facebook are trying, and the stage is set for a clash of epic proportions between the Internet giants.

Indeed, the age we live in right now is one where our friends are soon to be the tastemakers in our online lives, the curators of all the information we care about. Whereas the holy grail of online marketing has always been a #1 spot on Google, the new environment necessitates that your company become a popular topic of discussion on social networks as well. The currency of the Internet is changing from one based on links—the symbol of trust in the eyes of search engines—to a currency of likes, comments, pins, retweets, shares, and video responses. Simply put, virality is the new decider of business. Soon, we won't be looking for everything on Google as we do today. Instead, Google and Facebook will be actively suggesting things to us—often, things we never even knew we needed. Simply announce to the world that you have a cold, and you will find out that your colleague from work and your college roommate recommend Cold-eez, that your friend Danny likes an article about holistic cold remedies on WebMD.com, and that your mom is worried about you and wants you to come home.

While Google struggles to integrate these kinds of social recommendations into a platform that is slowly becoming a thing of the past—a traditional search engine— Facebook, the newer, cooler Internet giant, is at the cusp of technology, delivering social information directly to the profile page you keep open six hours per day, or better yet, through your mobile phone.

Indeed, the social search wars are on, and you, the consumer, need only sit back and watch. Before you know it, you'll be able to buy a drink for a friend who is across the country, get personalized movie recommendations whenever you're near a theater, and hear your college professor's description of a landmark simply by holding your phone up to it. An algorithm will understand not just your social preferences, but the preferences of the people you trust. You won't need to search for anything. You won't even need to think.

And yet, having all of this useful information at your fingertips will come with one small catch—the implicit duty to provide the same kind of recommendations to other people. Think of it this way: If your friends are always helping you out, don't you want to help them back? As the amount of personal information on the Internet grows, the leading companies in the social realm will be asking you to make that data useful to the people in your life. And then, predictably (but not as annoyingly as you would think), the same companies will use that information to advertise to you.

Telling your friends what you like, dislike, and recommend is a small price to pay for the incredible possibilities social data will introduce. Let me give you an example. If you were single and someone told you that they had found the ideal partner for you, who has many of the same interests as you, grew up in a similar town, and loves all of your favorite movies, wouldn't you jump on that opportunity? If I weren't married, I sure as hell would. What if you were looking for a job and someone told you that they had a friend of a friend who is the head of personnel at your favorite company? Wouldn't you be grateful?

Both of these examples are potential applications of the data that the world will be providing to Facebook, Google, Twitter, YouTube, Pinterest, and other Internet companies in the next few years. And the "someone" who keeps doing you these incredible favors is their next great innovation: social media.

What's In This Book?

This book consists of nine chapters that cover all the social media concepts and strategies you need to change the face of your business forever. The chapters are divided as follows:

- Chapter 1 describes the brewing war between Facebook and Google, why it matters to you, and how it has shaped the two websites we spend the majority of our time using. It also prepares you for all the material in the rest of the book.

- Chapter 2 illustrates the social landscape we are playing on today— where it is now and where it is quickly headed. This chapter explains how to build a massive audience on Facebook.

- Chapters 3 delves into the new ways we will be discovering information on the major social networks, and shows you how to use these paradigms to your advantage.

- Chapter 4 covers the sleeping giant of search: real-time search. It reveals why status updates matter and how you can use them to mine valuable data for your business.

- Chapter 5 discusses the best strategies for local businesses, outlining specific techniques that companies with a physical presence need to know.

- Chapter 6 gives you the best and most cutting-edge information available on translating social media into profits.

- Chapter 7 is a glimpse into the not-too-distant future. What will businesses need to be thinking about in 2017?

- Chapter 8 teaches you how to succeed with the most important advertising platform of the next five years: Facebook ads.

- Chapter 9 outlines the core strategies businesses need to harness the power of YouTube, LinkedIn, public speaking, and online reputation management.

Who Can Use This Book?

Outsmarting Social Media was written for the middle 80% of social media users. Total beginners—those who don't know what a tweet is or how to set up a Facebook page—might find this book a little over their heads. On the other side of the coin, those who are on the very cusp of new technology, reading all the tech publications and attending developer conferences in Silicon Valley, might find that they are already familiar with many of its concepts.

This book's ideal reader has a personal profile on Facebook as well as a business page; has a Twitter account, even if it is inactive; and uses search engines constantly. He is either a business owner or a marketer, with a desire to excel beyond his competitors using simple, commonsense tactics.

I will say that even if you are outside the target group—if you're a novice or a ninja—this book was written to be interesting and readable, and I promise that you will get something out of it.

Those who are reading this book hoping to learn how to trick social media sites or engage in "black hat" tactics should look elsewhere; my techniques are meant to last for the long term, withstanding algorithm changes, interface enhancements, and social media flavors of the week.

I am a firm believer that the best social media strategy is the most obvious: creating content with lasting value and sharing it consistently. However, it is not easy to conceive of all the ways to implement such a strategy, which is why you need this book. The product of years of trial and error, of success and failure, of epiphany and heartbreak, awaits you.

And while you're on your journey, know that I'm there with you. I respond to all email, and can be reached at evanmbailyn@gmail.com.

An Important Note

A lot of people have asked me how I could put out a book that reveals my best social media tactics and still remain in business. It is true that if every social media entrepreneur put my strategies into effect, I'd seem to have lost my unique offering. Doyle Brunson, one of the best poker players of all time, wrote a book on poker that was so widely studied that it opened up the game of poker to millions more people—many of whom ended up taking money from him at the tables. He later said he regretted writing the book.

Well, I don't know if this book will have the same effect on entrepreneurs, but I do have a bit of insurance: I know that very few people who read this book will actually do the work required to implement my techniques. Whether because of limited time, limited budget, or a subconscious fear of success, most people will admire good ideas but never actually do anything about them.

Despite this fact, I'm asking you to be a part of the group that does something with the knowledge in this book. I'm imploring you to push through the whirlwind of doubts and dismissals that say "I can't do that; It's too hard; It requires too much expertise that I don't have; It probably won't amount to anything anyway" and allow yourself to achieve more than you thought possible.

Every person reading this book has the opportunity to make their business thrive using only what is contained within. Some ideas might be new to you, but most will be easy to grasp. The decision to use the power of social media to your greatest benefit is yours to make—and I genuinely hope you take advantage of it.

1

The Clash of the Internet Giants

Back in 2007, Google was sitting pretty. It was the leading search engine in the United States by a large margin, its stock was soaring, and it was innovating at an incredible rate. The word "google" had long become an entry in the dictionary, and our culture had fully embraced the company. All roads seemed to be leading to Google.

Social networks were a big deal back then. MySpace was extremely popular, and Facebook was a rising star, especially among college kids and twentysomethings. Conveniently for Google, those sites had nothing to do with search. They were separate businesses altogether, whose main purpose was to connect people online. Any search functions they possessed were either rudimentary or, in the case of MySpace, handled by Google itself.

If someone were to predict that, within five years, Google's main competitor would be Facebook, people probably wouldn't understand how. Social networking and search seemed to be separated by a large chasm, sort of like news and shopping. The two were just...different.

Google's main competitors back then were Yahoo, MSN, and Ask. All were in the business of returning information to users based on searches, and all made money from advertising. The competitive landscape was easy to understand. Google was gaining market share every quarter, whereas Yahoo and MSN were losing market share (see Figure 1.1). Indeed, this was a great time for the Big G.

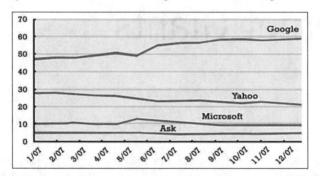

Figure 1.1   *A graph of the search market share in 2007, according to comScore.*

The situation continued in this way until late 2009, when Facebook started to be the one you heard about in the news the way you used to hear about Google from 2004 to 2007. Suddenly, Facebook was overtaking MySpace in popularity, getting valuations north of $1 billion, and introducing a mysteriously simple concept called "likes."

A funny thing was happening. Facebook was becoming the next big thing. And, far more than its predecessors, Friendster and MySpace, Facebook truly seemed set to change the Internet.

The Rise of Facebook

I wish I could tell you that I knew how important Facebook would become even a year before I decided to write this book. But I didn't. It kind of snuck up on me— on everyone, really. Here was Google, who had this hugely ambitious motto, "organizing the world's information"—and it was really doing it. It seemed everything it touched turned to gold, and it touched some incredible things.

Do you remember the first time you saw Google Earth, which opened with a satellite picture of the entire planet and then, within seconds, zoomed down into accurate pictures of your city, your neighborhood, even your *house*? Personally, I'll never forget reading about Google Books for the first time and marveling at the idea of millions of books being as easy to search through as any web page in Google's index. It made me recall, not without some queasiness, having to use the Dewey Decimal System to find sources for my book reports back in the seventh grade (remember those old cabinets they had in every library, with all the drawers filled with cards organized by "call numbers"?). Google was giving me easy access to all the data I could ever need, and I was impressed.

Compared to all of that, what was Facebook? It was really just a profile like the one I used to have on AOL in 1998, with a screen name, a list of interests, my favorite quote, and some pictures. Okay, so it was a supercharged profile, but not much more than that.

The first thing that alerted me to the fact that Facebook was a big deal was its sheer popularity. I kept reading about how tens of millions of people, and then hundreds of millions of people, were using it. And people were using it for huge amounts of time—up to 6 hours per day, which is far above the Internet average for a website of 1 to 2 minutes per day. When Facebook officially became bigger than MySpace, I realized that the company was worth watching. It seemed that people were starting to integrate it into their lives in a way similar to other cultural staples, like television. The fact that Microsoft and Yahoo were attempting to buy the company for billions of dollars didn't hurt my interest, either. But none of that was enough for me to truly realize Facebook's significance.

Reading about the "open graph" for the first time was the moment when I realized that Facebook was serious about influencing the world in a real way.

Facebook has an internal social graph, which is basically a huge map of how everyone on Facebook is connected to one another, as well as to their own interests. It is a visualization of your friendships and interests, and the ways in which your friendships and interests overlap with those of other people, both inside and outside your social circle. It could, for instance, tell you how many degrees of separation you are from Justin Bieber (hopefully, many).

Facebook's *open* social graph—the concept that bowled me over—is a map as well, but it involves one major new element: other websites. The open graph takes all that juicy data about who you're friends with and what you like and ports it to other websites so they can use it to create a more personalized experience. The results are fascinating.

At the most basic level, the open graph works like this: Imagine if websites knew as much about you as Facebook does. They could serve you a far more relevant experience. Let's say you enjoy hiking. It's Saturday, and you're on your favorite hiking website looking for a new trail. If this site were integrated with Facebook's open graph, it could potentially tell you the trails that you are most likely to enjoy based on your age, other trails you like, and input you've given to others about hiking. It could even tell you which trails your friends enjoy most. As a bonus, it could take into consideration the temperature, humidity, and pollen count. Your experience with this site just went from generic—that is, purely informational—to personal (see Figure 1.2).

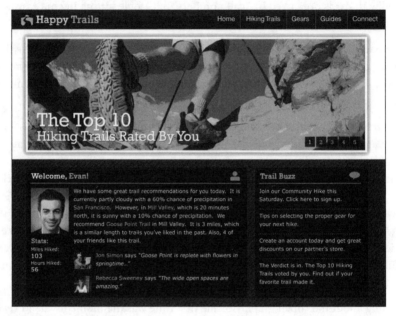

Figure 1.2 *An example of the way Facebook could influence our experience on web-sites. This hiking site utilizes social data and other available data in an intelligent way.*

When Mark Zuckerberg, the CEO of Facebook, announced the open graph in April 2010, he used three popular websites to help explain what the graph meant, and I think they demonstrate its importance:

- **CNN.com**—If you regularly visit this site, you know that there is so much news on the home page that it is difficult to read even just the *day's* highlights, let alone interesting stories you may have missed from yesterday or last week. However, with the open social graph plugged into CNN.com, you can now see which articles are the most popular among your friends. While you're on Facebook.com, you can also see which articles your friends like: whenever they "like" an article, that action is reported back to Facebook so it can be included in the stream of updates on your home screen.

- **IMDB.com**—Movies are one of the most common activities for which we seek outside opinions. How often have you sought out a friend's opinion about a movie before seeing it? At the very least, you probably read a review. This is why the IMDB.com integration with Facebook's open social graph is so cool (see Figure 1.3). When you're on the site looking at any movie page, you can see which of your friends like that movie. If you think the friends who like the movie share your taste, you very well may choose to see it. This is a great example of how social information can *drive purchases*—one of the reasons why social search and discovery are such exciting new technologies.

Figure 1.3   *IMDB.com's integration with Facebook's open graph: the site allows you to see which of your friends like any given movie, and it enables you to "like" movies yourself, which in turn makes that information available to your friends.*

- **Pandora.com**—Pandora is a website that functions like a personalized radio station based on your tastes. Put in a song you like and Pandora will find similar music, much of which you may never have heard, and play it for you, free of charge. It is an excellent way to discover and enjoy new music. Its integration with the open social graph allows users to see which songs their friends like, and you can contribute to that useful pool of information by clicking "like" on the songs that you enjoy. Even more conveniently—or eerily, depending on what you believe—you can look through your friends' favorite songs and radio stations, almost like you were back in the 1990s, browsing through their collection of CDs on the nifty new rack they purchased at Tower Records.

As you can see, the initial applications of social data to websites are pretty neat. The reason I am describing them here is to give you a picture of Facebook's ambitions. More than just a social network, Facebook is becoming a kind of standard fixture for all the websites on the Internet. If we liken the Internet to a community, Facebook doesn't want to be just a big entertainment complex; it wants to be the plumbing system that passes unnoticeably through every single house. It wants you to be relying on it all the time, even when you aren't thinking about it. Make no mistake about it—that kind of universality is what Mark Zuckerberg and his core staff spent most of their time thinking about in 2009, 2010, and 2011.

One reason it is so valuable to show up on as many websites as possible is data. Sure, Facebook wants to help personalize websites with its social data, making a better experience for Internet users. But far more than that, it wants to spy on us.

Now, I don't mean that in a conspiratorial way. I'm just trying to give a clear picture of what Facebook is really gaining by having its code embedded in hundreds of thousands of websites. When you are logged in to Facebook and surfing a site that has Facebook code on it, Facebook is collecting data about you. After all, it may know a lot about you, but Facebook can learn far more by observing which websites you visit and how you behave on those websites.

Facebook gets its code onto websites—and thus collects data about you—in many ways. The main ways in which it tempts webmasters to add Facebook code is by offering social plug-ins, such as Like buttons on the website; providing the capability to personalize the website with Facebook's open graph, as described previously in the CNN, IMDB, and Pandora examples; or allowing users to log in to the website using their Facebook credentials (otherwise known as the Facebook Connect program).

The data that Facebook is collecting by appearing in one form or another on so many websites is helping it catch up with Google, which has been doing the same thing for a while. Google incentivizes webmasters to add special code to their website using its Google Analytics and Adsense programs. But more on that later.

Google's Problem

At the end of the day, both Google and Facebook are advertising companies that depend on having your time and attention in order to sell their ad space. That two hours you spent on Facebook this morning? Google would have preferred you spent it on a Google property instead. If you had, you would have seen more of its ads and it would have made more money. That 45 minutes you spent watching Japanese game shows on YouTube during your lunch break? Facebook would have preferred you spent that time reading wall posts and browsing through pictures of your friends on Facebook. That way, it could have had your attention on *its* ads.

Boiling down what is becoming a battle of epic proportions to its simplest components— a competition for your ad-clicking potential—reminds me of a conversation I had with a board member back when I owned my kids website, Cartoon Doll Emporium. We were discussing whether to add an elaborate and expensive virtual world to the site. I knew little about virtual worlds at the time and was reluctant to do it.

I asked him, "Do we need to have one just because all of the other big companies in the space do?" His reply: "It doesn't matter if you have a virtual world or not. The only reason a virtual world is appealing is because it keeps people interested in the site longer. If you could keep people interested just as long with a celebrity blog, daily poetry contest, or—hell, by reprinting pages from the telephone book—you should do that instead. The content doesn't matter; what matters is getting people hooked."

I think his point is correct. When a company makes its money from advertising, time and attention is all that matters. With Google, we have a company that has gained your time and attention by being the most incredible information retrieval resource on Earth, a company that is now realizing that people are more inter-ested in the mundane activities of their friends than in the sum total of everything Google has spent billions of dollars to create. Make no mistake—Google is jealous. Suddenly, something *other than search* became so integral to people's online lives that they spend hours each day doing it.

To be fair, Google is far from blind to the power of social expression on the Net. Its YouTube acquisition, even at the premium price of $1.8 billion, was a crucial move. Besides the obvious benefits of video as searchable data, YouTube is an increasingly important way that people communicate with one another. Google has also been resolute in its advancement of its own social product, Google+, even going so far as integrating its status updates into search results. However, it remains to be seen whether users will embrace search results that are personalized by a social network they rarely use and a browsing history they never meant to share.

Facebook, on the other hand, is as good at social as Google is at search, and that makes Facebook a huge threat. From Google's perspective, there are three distinct reasons to feel intimidated by Facebook:

- **Google will never be better than Facebook at offering a social experience to users.** When I think about Google's main strength—organizing tera-bytes of data and delivering relevant bits of it to you in seconds using a brilliant algorithm—it also highlights Google's main weakness: under-standing the human side of the Internet.

  I once had a chat with a former classmate of Google co-founder Larry Page. "Larry was always a robot," he told me. "He believes he can solve every problem with an algorithm."

  If we take this person's observation at face value, it's not surprising that the very DNA of Google is algorithm based. Facebook's DNA, on the other hand, comes from a guy who—according to personal accounts and at least one Academy Award-winning movie—started Facebook to get girls. As such, I am willing to bet that Facebook will always be great at providing users with a social experience, and Google will lag behind in that area. Google will instead have to focus on organizing social information from multiple sources, Facebook among them, and serv-ing it to users in relevant ways.

- **Facebook knows much more about its users than Google does.** When you do a Google search, you are transmitting to Google only two pieces of data: your location, and what you're looking for. Unless you are a hardcore Google+ or YouTube user, or arrange all your social engagements through Gmail, Google has a limited amount of social data with which to serve relevant ads to you.

  When you log in to Facebook, on the other hand, you are constantly sharing information that reveals who you are: your real name; the names of your friends and family; the depth of your interest in each friend and family member; your age; your relationship status; your favorite movies, books, and music; and much more. On a personal level, Facebook knows you about as well as a computer script can know someone. Google, on the other hand, is probably only familiar with the more formal side of you—your researching and buying habits.

- **Facebook is beating Google in the battle to represent your social identity.** As the Web becomes more social, we have begun to require a way to represent ourselves on various websites without having to log in to each one of them. Classically, social interaction on the Internet has been anonymous. In Web 1.0, we had forums, where you picked a username and maybe a picture to go with it, and that became your identity. In Web 2.0, we have lots of social sites, but most of them do not require real information (check out "Fake Steve Jobs"). In Web 3.0, there will be less anonymity than ever, as the rise of Facebook has heralded a movement toward tying your real identity to social interaction. Websites, no doubt, love it because it gives them more information on their visitors, keeps people on their best behavior, and generally improves the quality of conversation. Eventually, most big sites will require users to log in if they want to partake in the discussion.

  This presents a fascinating revenue opportunity for both Google and Facebook. You see, whichever site becomes the default sign-in for most of the big websites will also be lurking around when you are purchasing something at one of those sites. Being present at the point of purchase is only a hop away from *participating* in that purchase. While you're logged in to Facebook, why not click one button and pay for your purchase using Facebook, too (see Figure 1.4)? Similarly, if you're already logged in to your Google account, it would be easy to use Google's payment solution. The key to this whole thing is, the company that helps you pay always gets a small percentage of the purchase price, either from the buyer or seller. So there is 1% or so in it for whoever wins this brewing battle.

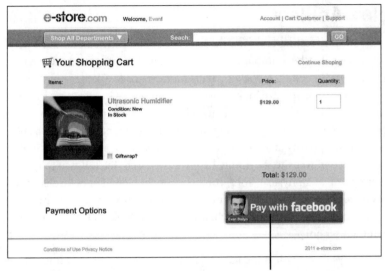

This is a mock-up of how Facebook
could be part of online purchases

Figure 1.4 *The potential Facebook payment solution. It would be an easy transition from personalization partner to payment partner.*

Now, which site will users choose? The answer goes back to the concept of identity. Of the two sites, which one do you trust to always have running in the background, to be the filter through which you socialize online? Because Facebook is already tied into your social identity so closely, it has the clear advantage.

Google knows this, but it will not allow Facebook to win the identity battle without a fight. That is why we have seen Google profiles start to show up at the top of the results when you search for a person's name: Google is seeking to become synonymous with your identity. Identity is also what Google+ is all about. A late entry into the social networking game, Google+ was conceived to become a staple of people's lives just like email, inducing them to store all of their personal info on the site, from social connections to bank account details. Currently, it is masquerading as just a social network, but the ambitions behind it—gaining a payload of social data about each of us and our connections—belie Google's grander goals.

I doubt Google will win this battle though, as it has never succeeded at being a highly personal company, and the concepts of identity and payment are both quite personal. Equally importantly, Facebook is an ambitious company that has a huge head start at being the de facto social destination.

Google's Artillery

In case you were feeling bad for Google, it should be pointed out that even though Google envies the sheer amount of time, attention, and personal information people give to Facebook, Google's data is more valuable. Google points you to specific websites when you are looking to buy something—in effect, referring more business to online companies than any other entity on earth. That is a very powerful position. Whether you're looking to buy something, navigating to a specific website, or just poking around for ideas, Google is there to suggest a vendor, serve you your desired website, or simply help you research. Even if you're going to buy something at a physical store, you are likely to Google it beforehand. When it comes down to it, Google is there for you when you need to do anything economic. And Facebook? It's there for you when you need to look up that girl you used to date in high school.

In many ways, Facebook is the Lady Gaga to Google's Madonna. It is a fresh, incredibly popular upstart that people expect a lot from in the future. But it hasn't proven itself time and time again like Google has. Compare Lady Gaga, who has a newness and bravado about her that amounts to a certain "coolness," with Madonna, who has the wisdom of a career-long hitmaker. So, too, goes the story of Facebook and Google.

Let's not forget the bottom line, either. Facebook made $4 billion in 2011. Google made more than $37 billion. When you have that much money, you can do things that a company Facebook's size could not even dream of doing. This is the same advantage Microsoft has classically had over Google. Although Google has probably never been worried that Microsoft would create a better search engine, Google probably has been worried that someone, somewhere in the world *would* create one and Microsoft would buy it. Heck, Microsoft could have even bought some of the infrastructure that Google relies on.

A good illustration of the benefits of Google's piggy bank occurred back in 2007 when Google competed against Verizon and AT&T in a government auction for a rare and desirable part of the wireless spectrum. The wireless spectrum is the network that allows cell phone companies to provide phone service. Winning the auction would have effectively made Google into a wireless service provider. Being able to provide Internet access to tens of millions of people would have sewn Google's presence into the very fabric of the wireless Internet, giving it numerous competitive advantages against other search engines. The price tag for this item ended up being $4.74 billion. Although Google did not win (it was about a hundred million dollars behind Verizon), its ability to participate in the auction changed the rules of wireless access permanently, paving the way for Android cell phones to become as popular as they are today.

Now *that's* a big-boy move. Even after its IPO, Facebook is still behind Google in its ability to make such seismic business decisions.

Equally significant is Google's head start on Facebook in terms of the universality of presence on websites, which I discussed in the previous section. Having Google ads on millions of websites for many years has given it a stack of data that is miles high. Google's use of this information, along with its core search data, to perfect its advertising program is what has made Google so much money, and what will continue to give it an edge over Facebook in driving people to make purchases.

The Coming Showdown

Despite Google's current advantages, it is Facebook's *potential* that fascinates investors and the public alike. What will it do with all that social data? Will it change the way we discover new products and services? Will its ad product become so personalized that we begin to enjoy advertising? Will it alter the way humans interact in a way we never could have imagined?

As Facebook plots its way toward domination of the Internet's social future, Google is springing into action. When Larry Page took over as CEO of Google in April 2011, his first order was to tie 25% of every Google employee's bonus to the success of Google's social strategy. His message: if social fails, we all pay.

As with any two companies that have similar long-term goals and are constantly compared, Google and Facebook are deeply competitive. When it first became apparent that Facebook was a company with far-ranging potential, Google made some hasty moves to embrace social. One of the first, enacted in December 2009, was Realtime search, which allowed people to search through status updates that were posted moments ago (see Figure 1.5). At first, the only significant set of status updates Google could get its hands on was Twitter's. This made for a nice-looking, but ultimately useless product, because people could perform the same search on Twitter.com. (Google's Realtime search also included status updates from MySpace and Google Buzz, but both platforms had a negligible number of status updates compared to Twitter.)

Click Realtime   A limited number of social status updates are shown

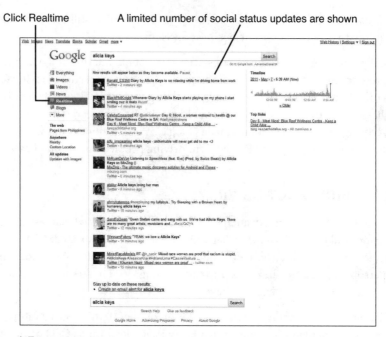

Figure 1.5 *Google's Realtime search product in mid-2011. Note that every result in this search came from Twitter. Facebook's huge bank of status updates was noticeably missing.*

In February 2011, Google's Realtime search got a boost when Google got its hands on a small slice of Facebook's status updates: the ones from public pages owned by companies, celebrities, and brands. Of course, the majority of status updates on Facebook are written on private profiles, so a major piece of the puzzle remained missing. Now, Facebook could have granted Google access to the status updates of its hundreds of millions of users. But it specifically chose not to. Instead, it handed that access over to Google's biggest search competitor, Bing. Finally, in June 2011, Twitter and Google ended their partnership, forcing Google to suspend its real-time search service and leaving them without any major allies in the social space.

Facebook's choosing to give its valuable social data—for free, no less—to one major search engine over the other was a slap in the face. Additionally, by giving Bing its "like" data, Facebook also allowed Bing to create the first true social search, a filter that causes websites your friends have "liked" to show up on the first page of the search results for relevant searches.

With both real-time search and social search basically handed to Bing by Facebook, Google was left to stew in its rejection. It had very much been the Queen Bee, the popular girl in high school who is used to getting everything she wants, until a new girl came to school and rose to an even greater popularity—and then dissed her in front of the whole cafeteria!

Google's reaction to Facebook's snub was never publicly disclosed, but one can only guess that more than a few naughty words were uttered inside Google's executive offices. The thing is, there was not too much Google could have done about it by way of retaliation. The two companies do not partner with each other on anything significant enough to give Google leverage. In fact, the only major thing that Google has over Facebook is its presence in Google's search results. However, removing Facebook from search results would be firmly against Google's policies and would result in a serious backlash from the public.

One minor thing that Google could have taken away from Facebook is access to the conduit (called an *API*) that allows Facebook users to invite their Gmail contacts to be friends on Facebook.

"If Google blocked Facebook's access to the Gmail address book, it would cause a lot of inconvenience for Facebook," Dustin Wittle, a former Yahoo engineer, told me. "Many people on Facebook find friends by using the feature that automatically searches through their Google contacts. If Google blocked that feature, new users would build up a base of friends a lot slower, which makes them less likely to get hooked on Facebook."

Still, even if Google did take this retaliatory action (and it has, but only in India), it is unlikely Facebook would just bow down. The company is simply too cocky, and more importantly, probably can live just fine without it.

With the reality of its lack of access to valuable Facebook data acknowledged, Google was left with a hard decision. Should it keep trying to strike some sort of partnership with Facebook, or attempt to manufacture its own social data?

Google chose the latter, debuting Google+ in June 2011. Although the service grew rapidly in its first few months, its usage was limited to mostly men and technically-oriented people. And though it has yet to go mainstream, Google is giving it the resources it needs to grow; sources inside Google tell me that the company is in it for the long haul and will continue to hone and improve Google+ over time.

It still remains to be seen whether Facebook will eventually share social data with Google. I asked many people inside Silicon Valley what they thought would happen and got very few decisive answers. Some ventured that Facebook would eventually hand it over, but was strengthening its bargaining position by giving Google a taste of what it's like to live without it (while its main competitor enjoys its advantages). Others believed that Facebook would never hand over the data, as that would be akin to ceding a major strategic advantage to a rival.

Personally, I think that Facebook will eventually share some data with Google as it becomes clear that neither company can socially curate the world's information without the other one. Both companies stand to benefit if they can strike the right deal.

As Facebook gains more and more social data, it is in a position to create the first true social search engine, one that finds websites, products, and services for searchers based on their social network and interests. It would be very useful to have Google power such a search, given that Google understands the search itself—that is, what people tend to be looking for when they type words into a box—better than anyone. The combination of a search engine that knows *what you are looking for* (Google) and *who you are* (Facebook) would be an incredible resource and monetization opportunity. Call it Foogle.

In short, although I'm not sure exactly how Google and Facebook will end up working together, I am certain that they will in a way that emphasizes each of the companies' obvious strengths. Google will not be able to dominate social by itself, and Facebook will not be able to dominate search by itself, so they will need to rely on each other.

2

The New Influences in Search and Social Media

As we move away from the pre-2010 world where everyone saw the same results for a given search on Google, we can reflect on what a silly proposition that was. The idea that a single answer could exist that satisfies all people is an antiquated concept, one that relies too heavily on a one-size-fits-all philosophy. If I, a California resident, typed "heat wave" into Google, I would probably be referring to the weather event, whereas if my best friend, a DJ who lives in Brooklyn, typed it in, he would probably be referring to the 1963 Motown song. For decades, our society has been pushing toward technology that truly "knows" its user. Today, we are at a unique moment in history where this possibility is close to becoming a reality—online, at least. Because we have not yet perfected artificial intelligence, we rely on algorithms to solve our problems. Algorithms have their limits, but now they have a new data set that is making them more powerful than ever: social data.

The Evolution of a Social Algorithm

If we think of Google's search algorithm as a river that used to get its water from a few select tributaries, it is now, with the addition of social data, receiving water from millions more tributaries, each with completely unique ingredients that change the composition of the river. The Google results page of tomorrow may still have 10 results and a bunch of ads, but those results will be personalized to the searcher based on her likes and interests and the likes and interests of others, both inside and outside her social network.

Figure 2.1 depicts a diagram that illustrates how I believe search results will look in 2014.

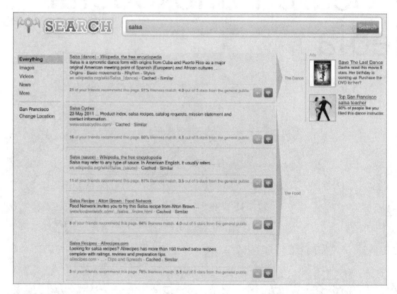

Figure 2.1 *My vision for how a Google results page might look in 2014.*

Whereas Google's method of ranking search results for a given query used to rely mostly on the meta page title (HTML code that denotes what the page is about) and number of links pointing to each page in its resultset, it now factors in the pages you and your friends have shared, discussed, and "+1ed." In a way, Google used to be like a scholarly professor who answers questions as if speaking from the textbook. The company is striving to be more like a knowledgeable friend who listens carefully to you and answers questions in the context of who you are.

Like the rapidly evolving Google results page, Facebook's user experience will be very different within a few years—from the "stream" of updates in the News Feed to the advertisements to the local offerings like Deals. Although Facebook has always been a personalized experience, it will soon be making more and more sophisticated suggestions: who to be friends with, what products to buy, which movies to watch, even which doctors to see. All these recommendations will come from what Facebook has learned about you and your friends.

The Rise of Tastemakers on Facebook

Although Google is groping for that highly desirable social data, Facebook is bathing in it. Because Facebook knows so much about you and your friends already, it is experimenting with new ways of serving relevant information to you. Facebook says it's to create a better social experience, but it's also for the money.

One of the most important innovations Facebook is working on right now is identifying who influences you the most. This intimate piece of information was not possible to determine algorithmically until this moment in history, when people do as much socializing online as they do in real life. Facebook is on the cusp of re-creating that age-old fashion archetype: the trendsetter.

> "Although Google is groping for that highly desirable social data, Facebook is bathing in it."

Trendsetters—or tastemakers, as I like to call them—are the people in your online social circle whose opinions matter the most to you. You know that friend who always manages to have the right clothes, or the one who has the most enviable travel experiences? These are the people you will be hearing the most from in the future. In fact, I predict that in a few years' time, a handful of your friends will have a bigger influence on your spending behavior than all the advertising you come into contact with. These people will *become* the new advertising. Sound annoying? Actually, it may not be so bad. A system as organic as getting recommendations from friends has its roots in a natural part of human behavior.

The tastemaker concept comes down to this: sharing opinions is fun. If your buddy asked for your thoughts about your cell phone because he was thinking about buying the same one, wouldn't you do your best to be helpful? In all likelihood, you'd give him even more information than he needed. Why? It feels good to be an expert in the eyes of the people you care about. It appeals to the part of you that wants to be heard. Do you remember those surveys that used to get passed around on AOL in the late 1990s? The ones that asked you random questions about yourself like "Have you ever kissed someone in the rain? Smiled for no reason? Laughed so hard you cried?" Millions of people answered every question on those surveys and then sent them around to all their friends, waiting patiently for that addictive "You've got mail" voice the next time they signed on. There's a reason stuff like that is popular—people love to talk about themselves.

Of course, certain people enjoy opining about things more than others do. The friends who always have a new restaurant to clue you in about, a great book that you just *have* to read, or a hilarious video you absolutely must watch are more likely to influence your purchases. These people are like the concierges of your social circle.

My brother Russell is a tastemaker in my social circle. I am constantly hearing about cool new restaurants, hot nightclubs, and fascinating people from him. Because he is so much like me, I often share his enthusiasm about the things he recommends. I trust his opinion so much that I call him up whenever I need an idea for a night out.

Russell, of course, is not an expert on everything I care about. By day he's a wealth manager, and by night he's a man about town, so I'd call his areas of expertise finance, nightlife, and entertainment. If I needed a book recommendation, I wouldn't call him, as he would probably recommend a book by some economist who speaks a language I don't understand. My mother-in-law, however, has an uncanny ability to pick out books that I absolutely love. Still other experts exist in my life in various categories: Rozzy and Brett for travel, my dad for legal advice, Jon for music, and Stephanie for wedding planning.

I relish thinking about the day when I can have all my trusted connections' advice in my pocket, taking their recommendations with me wherever I go. A list of Russell's Top 10 New York Restaurants or Rozzy's Best Hotels in France would be incredibly useful at the right moment. After Facebook has gathered enough data on our social actions, this type of information will soon be at our fingertips.

Facebook is kind of like a celebrity magazine where your friends are the celebrities. It seems obvious that if you are interested enough to read about what your friends are doing, you are probably also interested in their recommendations. Celebrity magazines often have a "Get So-And-So's Look!" feature that displays a bunch of products that will supposedly make you look like a particular celebrity. Tastemakers will be used in the same way. A friend who is known to have good taste in a certain area will offer, through Facebook, the chance to be like him or her. Off the bat, it sounds like a win-win situation because both advertisers and people will like it.

Let's say you've got a friend, Zach, who you think has excellent taste in clothing. Zach happens to wear a lot of Diesel jeans. If I were Facebook and I got my hands on this information, I'd be running to Diesel to ask if they'd like to advertise to everyone Zach is friends with who considers him a good dresser. That advertisement would be a simple story, maybe with a picture of Zach in Diesel jeans, that says: "Zach likes Diesel jeans. Buy a pair now at www.diesel.com." Maybe it would even list the nearest store that sells those jeans (see Figure 2.2). This would be an early version of social discovery, which I address more fully in the next chapter.

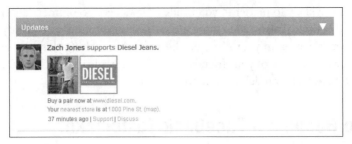

Figure 2.2   *Expect to see stories like these, which recommend products your friends like, in the near future.*

The trick—the thing that will truly make certain people influence others—is affinity. How close am I to Zach? More importantly, how much do I actually trust Zach's opinion about jeans? The way for this advertising technique to backfire is if the friends featured in the ads were not true tastemakers in the category the ad is targeting. It would be like a celebrity magazine trying to sell hair products to you by telling you they'll give you Donald Trump's look.

Facebook launched a social ad product called Deals in April 2011, and it utilizes an early version of the tastemaker concept. In the Deals section, offers from local merchants are featured with a note above each offer that tells you which friends like the products in those deals. But it lacks the affinity factor. It tells me, for instance, that my friend Mari likes a particular playhouse. But *I* don't care much for plays. And Mari has never struck me with her play-picking prowess. So the deal falls flat.

To determine who influences you the most in a particular area of interest, Facebook has begun categorizing your friends into groups in a more serious manner. In October 2010, Facebook simplified its groups to make it easier to add friends and receive notifications when there is activity in the group. It also placed groups more prominently on the sidebar. Eleven months later, in September 2011, Facebook made a small but crucial change: When you request someone as a friend, the pop-up menu immediately asks you whether the person is a close friend or an acquaintance. This small distinction helps Facebook understand whose

"Facebook is inching closer to being able to categorize each one of your friends based on their role in your life, which will make its advertising model much more successful."

story is more likely to matter to you inside a News Feed recommendation or an ad. Around this time, it also added more granular options for how frequently you want to see friends' stories in your News Feed. Facebook is inching closer to being able to categorize each one of your friends based on their role in your life, which will make its advertising model much more successful.

How to Become a Facebook Tastemaker

After Facebook figures out who your greatest influencers are in various categories—and it will, whether it starts asking people or keeps slogging along algorithmically—attracting the attention of these tastemakers will become your newest marketing objective. The strategy of pandering to trendsetters has been around forever and has traditionally existed in the realm of PR: get a celebrity to wear your product, and your sales will skyrocket. But you never see publicists following around rotary club presidents or heads of the PTA and asking them to wear clients' products. Soon, the equivalent of doing so will become standard for Facebook marketers. People who are known to be influential in their respective social circles will begin to get tons of Facebook messages and emails asking them to mention companies or products. Marketing power will fragment, shifting from the few celebrities that are most sought after to the average persons who are influential in their group. The theory of the *long tail*, which holds that selling less of a larger number of items is more valuable than selling more of just a few items, will come into play: marketing to a larger number of unknown people who are tastemakers in their group of friends will be more valuable than marketing to a small number of famous people.

And so, as businesspeople, how will we influence the influencers? The easiest way is to pay them, of course, but if that is your plan you wouldn't have bought this book. To unravel the answer, let's go back to high school. I often use high school as a context for thinking about marketing techniques because the foundation of so many of our later behaviors lies in adolescence. Also, high school is a time when the feelings people have—both positive and negative—are particularly dramatized.

If you were a regular guy and wanted to get the attention of the popular group, what would you do? Doing their homework wouldn't work, because it would only lead to them walking all over you. Trying too hard to fit in would come across as unnatural and end up embarrassing you. Even being straightforward would likely fail because, well, high school is all about social class. And therein lies the key: If you want to influence popular people, you need to become popular yourself.

Becoming popular on Facebook allows you to reach a large number of people with your marketing messages, including tastemakers who may pass your recommendations on to their friends. It also helps you earn the respect of tastemakers who, recognizing your status, will be more open to cross-promotion and other business development deals.

To achieve fame on Facebook, you will need to have a business page. If your company doesn't already have one, it is not using Facebook properly. A business page, as opposed to a personal profile, allows you to have an infinite number of fans—technically called "likes"—and promote your commercial interests. A personal profile limits you to 5,000 friends and does not allow any business promotion.

When you have your business page set up, you will want to start attracting as many likes as possible. These people are your fan base, and you can message them anytime by updating your status, which in turn appears in their News Feed. Fans vary in their value to your company. Some will ignore, or even block, your updates, and others may engage actively with your page. The hope is that some of your active fans will be tastemakers and will influence others to "like" your page. It's all about numbers: Mathematically speaking, some small percentage of your fans will be tastemakers. And so, the more fans you have, the more tastemakers you will have acquired.

The following sections explain the three best ways I know to become massively popular on Facebook.

Build an Organic Fan Base

When I first started a public page for myself on Facebook, I wasn't even quite sure what I was doing. I just started with the simple idea of saying *only* things that came directly from my heart. Those status updates could have been about Google or Facebook or something else I make money from, but my first instinct was to talk about the importance of believing in yourself. I did so because I could talk about that topic with more sincerity than any other. Within one year, I went from having a fan base of a few dozen of my friends to having the largest number of fans of any noncelebrity on Facebook, numbering over 100,000. More important than the numbers is the fact that I have a built-in marketing channel for all my companies. Beyond that, I have also made relationships with other tastemakers who promote my brand for free because they want me to promote theirs.

How did I get there? Well, it was part natural and part marketing savvy, as all popular things seem to be. Let's go back to the days when I had fewer than 100 "likes" on Facebook. I got the initial base by suggesting my page to all 350 of my friends at the time. I then sent personal messages to all the friends I knew had a lot of friends themselves—the tastemakers of my group. My message would look something like the one in Figure 2.3.

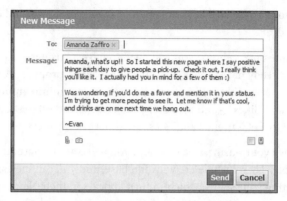

Figure 2.3 *An example of the kind of message that worked for getting my popular friends to promote my page for free.*

Writing to about 10 friends, 4 of which were happy to mention my page, brought my numbers up to 600 in one week. Having earned a reasonably sized fan base on merit—after all, they didn't have to click "like" on my page unless they saw something interesting about it—I felt confident that my method was working. In business, when you see a marketing method work, you push on it all you can. Knowing that I was about to embark on a campaign of writing to people and asking them to mention my page as those four awesome people already had, I wanted to improve my conversion percentage. In other words, I wanted more of the people who clicked my page to decide to "like" it. My interesting quotes weren't quite enough to rope certain people in; they needed some cajoling. That's when I decided to implement a landing tab, one of the best things you can do for your business page.

A landing tab on Facebook is a page that everyone who doesn't already "like" your page sees when they first visit your page. As of March 2012, Facebook users can only see a landing tab when they arrive from a Facebook ad. A landing tab can have anything you want on it, but it should always accomplish two things:

1. Welcome people

2. Ask them to "like" your page

I decided to welcome people by telling them the quick story of who I am, and I asked them to "like" my page by using a squiggly red arrow (see Figure 2.4).

Figure 2.4   *My Facebook landing page, complete with a welcome cartoon and a squiggly red arrow asking people to "like" my page.*

With a landing page to aid me in gaining likes, I embarked on a message-writing spree, using both Facebook and email, that converted people at almost twice the rate as before. The page was doing its job. By the time I had 1,200 likes, I found that the organic effect was kicking in. Every day, about 5 new people would like the page, even when I hadn't gotten a mention that day. That's when having a good page counts. I could have let the page grow naturally from there, but I wouldn't be much of an optimizer if I did that, now would I?

Having run out of contacts to ask the favor from, I began emailing random popular people on Facebook, telling them that I wanted to do a trade with them. If they mentioned me on their page—a two-second thing that their fans would thank them for anyway!—I would either perform a small SEO service for them for free, give them a mention on my page, or, if neither of those appealed to them, pay them. I think I offered around $20. Believe it or not, a bunch of people were interested.

Let me pause for a minute here to say that, if it seems like I was just having success after success, that is not what it felt like at the time. I was getting ignored or called nasty names far more than I was getting my offers accepted, but I kept at it.

Three months into my email writing campaign, I reached a tipping point: With 3,200 likes, I now had enough of a fan base that I could reasonably offer these popular people—many of whom had about the same number of friends as I had fans—a status update in response. Although I had been offering this the whole time, it was not desirable until I had a few thousand likes. Suddenly people were warming to the idea. I would estimate that about 1 in 10 people I contacted were okay with the idea. Keep in mind that these people were probably more likely to do the deal with me because they saw my page was positive and noncommercial. For that reason, if you use this method, it may be best to build a fan base around advice-giving or something else genuine before commercializing your page. Otherwise, you're likely to see the number of people who want to mention you to their friends go down to 1 in 100.

Continuing my campaign, I finally cracked the 10,000 likes mark, and from there my page grew organically, getting nearly 50 new likes per day. The lessons here:

- Start a Facebook page that people genuinely like.
- Use your network of friends to promote that page.
- Don't be too commercial, especially at first, or you'll risk turning potential "likers" off.
- Be bold enough to contact people outside your social network.
- Consistency is key when doing a marketing outreach; when you see something working, keep it going no matter how much discouragement you encounter.

Although there are undoubtedly many other ways to become a popular figure on Facebook, you will always need good status updates and a thorough amount of marketing outreach, especially in the beginning. Don't be afraid of that work; it's not that bad, and it's the barrier that keeps out almost everyone else. If you can stick with it for a few months, you are likely to be the rare person who gains a large, active following.

Entertain People to Increase Exposure to Your Status Updates

Beyond just being a gossip feed, Facebook is also a daily digital newspaper. People get up in the morning, read the headlines of what their friends are up to, and try to find something interesting to start off their day. Later on, they go back and check the latest headlines, hoping for a pleasant distraction from their responsibilities. The amount of attention that people pay to their Facebook News Feeds is incredible, and it creates an opening for a marketer: entertain them!

No matter what your profession is, it is a good idea to create a daily entertaining status update that relates to your industry. If it's good enough, people will begin to look forward to it, commenting, sharing, and "liking" it abundantly each day. Facebook takes note of pages with high-engagement status updates and rewards them with top placement on people's News Feeds. The end result of being "admitted" to the top of your fans' News Feeds is that, not only will your fun updates get a lot of attention, but so will your promotional updates. Being the popular guy opens doors for you to promote your business. Or, to put it another way, owning the entertainment means free advertising.

There are many ways to entertain your fans using your status updates. One way, if we continue to look at Facebook like a newspaper, is to become the Funnies page. If you posted a daily cartoon relating to your business, I have no doubt it would be met with intrigue.

Now you may be saying to yourself: "I sell cell phone accessories. Why am I going to spend my time making cartoons for people and posting them on Facebook?" And to that I would ask you "Have you ever seen a company that sells cell phone accessories doing that?" Probably not. Yours would stand out in people's minds. If you don't believe it can be done, see Figure 2.5.

"This hands-free cell phone has really made my driving safer!""

Figure 2.5 *You can make entertaining content for your company no matter what kind of business it is. Posting this kind of content through your Facebook business page leads to more exposure for your status updates—and not just to the fun ones, but to your promotional updates as well.*

If creating something from scratch on a daily, or even weekly, basis intimidates you, there are other things you can do to increase your fans' engagement that require less effort. Here are a few of the most popular kinds of status updates:

- **News story commentary**—This is a fairly simple technique if you've got even the slightest bit of snark in you. Look for current news in your field that is somewhat ridiculous, post the link as your status, and accompany it with a sarcastic comment. You could even seek out articles on "weird news" sites if you want to make the fishing easier (see Figure 2.6). People love a kooky news story because it's true, and if you manage to strike just the right tone of irony in your comment, people will interact a lot.

Figure 2.6 *A snarky comment next to a ridiculous news article: an ideal way to increase engagement with your Facebook page's status updates without expending too much time or effort.*

You do not need to be sarcastic if that's not your style. A sincere comment like "Wow, this is insane!" could also work just fine.

- **The day's best video**—Another easy way to engage fans is to find popular videos on YouTube. Although many people look at YouTube daily, you can be sure that not all of your Facebook friends do. Therefore, that brand-new viral video, which can be conveniently found at the top of YouTube's Most Viewed page each day, is great fodder for a post. Accompany it with a comment, and you've got some engaging content right out of the box.

- **Popular wisdom**—Everybody loves a good quote—succinct and powerful. Pick one that relates to your industry from one of the hundreds of quote websites out there and post away. If you can further relate the quote to something going on that day, people will be even more tempted to comment.

- **Easy Questions**—As we learned in the beginning of this chapter, sharing opinions is fun for everyone. The easiest way to elicit these opinions is to ask an open question. Facebook has a Questions icon you can click to get a formatted question interface with the answers listed like survey results. Or you can just ask within your regular status update. When deciding on a question, remember to stick to things that are simple to answer and not too personal. That will get you the maximum number of responses. For instance, I've found that asking people what cell phone service they have and how they like it is one of the most tame and popular things you can put out there. People usually have an opinion on their phone service, and it doesn't require them to trip over any privacy barriers to answer it. Other great categories are favorite foods, top vacation spots, cute pet stories, and nostalgic musings (see Figure 2.7).

Figure 2.7   *Simple, fun questions lead to lots of answers.*

If you do decide to become a popular status updater—and I hope you do—just keep in mind that you are doing so from a business page. (Incidentally, all this advice applies equally well to your personal status updates, but that's not what this book is about.) Although you have license to be lighthearted because, after all, you are on Facebook, a *social* platform, not LinkedIn or some other business platform, you still want to strike a tone that matches the professionalism of your company. Also, be sure to post sparingly. If you get too update-happy, people will block your updates, causing the opposite effect of what you were trying to accomplish. It is best to post two status updates maximum per day.

Follow these guidelines, and you will find your way into countless News Feeds, skyrocketing your business page's popularity.

Facebook Ads

Earning "likes" and engagement organically is a crucial skill to learn, but it is equally important to know how to advertise properly on Facebook. That is a strong statement coming from an optimizer who likes to beat the system rather than paying retail. But the beauty of Facebook ads is, if you understand how to run them properly, you can pay a tiny fraction of what the average person pays and earn likes in less time than it would take to complete an organic campaign like the one I did for my page. Although an organic campaign still tends to bring fans who are more interested in your page from the start (a friend's recommendation is more powerful than an advertisement), advertising can still bring its fair share of tastemakers to your page. And tastemakers, of course, are the drivers of organic engagement on Facebook.

Setting up an advertising campaign on Facebook is so much less complicated than setting one up on Google that it seems Google should take a cue from Facebook. Okay, fine, Google made tens of billions of dollars from its complicated ad platform, but if it wants to make more, I think Google should consider the simplicity of Facebook's ad interface, which can be understood by almost anyone on the first try.

After you have set up your account and put your credit card number on file, you have to set up a campaign. There are several variables to consider in your campaign in terms of which Facebook users you are targeting:

> "I think Google should consider the simplicity of Facebook's ad interface, which can be understood by almost anyone on the first try."

- Age
- Gender
- Location
- Relationship Status
- Interests
- Education
- Workplace
- Whether someone is already a fan of your page

This kind of laser demographic targeting may seem like a marketer's dream—and it is. People take for granted that, before Facebook ads came out, this type of targeting precision simply didn't exist, neither in traditional nor in online advertising. If Google were capable of giving its advertisers this level of targeting, it would severely cripple Facebook's ability to make money. As it stands, psychographic targeting is Facebook's key advantage over Google, whereas commercial intentionality targeting—the ability to advertise to people who are looking to buy a particular item—is Google's main advantage (see Figure 2.8).

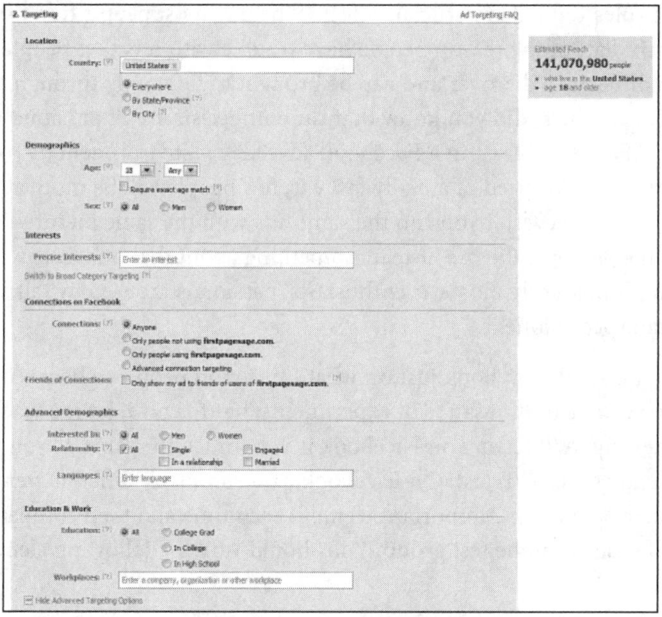

Figure 2.8   *The targeting section on the Facebook ads interface.*

When using Facebook ads to build a large fan base, whom you target is key. The cardinal rule is this: The greater the percentage of people in your targeted group that interact with your ad, the less you will pay for each interaction. This means you should not target extremely broad categories of people, such as 18- to 35-year-old males unless you can think of an ad that is enticing to virtually every 18- to 35-year-old male (I'll let your mind wander there). Rather, you should go after smaller groups of people who all have something important in common.

A typical Facebook ad consists of a picture along with 2 or 3 sentences. You should use your limited real estate to accomplish three things, which I call the Rules of Creating a Successful Facebook Ad:

1. Get people to identify with the ad.

2. Interest people by appealing to something they are not just interested in, but are passionate about.

3. Ask them explicitly to perform an action.

Although rules 1 and 3 are crucial, rule 2 is the one most people don't successfully accomplish. Part of the reason people have trouble with it is that people's passions are often difficult to discover and can be brought to light only through extensive testing. For instance, did you know that car enthusiasts aren't passionate about the speed of a car? At least in a Facebook advertising environment, if you run ads mentioning the top speed of a really fast car, few people will be motivated enough to click on it. However, if you run the same ads with the same pictures, except mention the *power* of the car instead, something about that one little word changes everything. Apparently most car enthusiasts' passion is aroused by talk of power rather than speed alone.

I could write a different book just on what I've found people to be passionate about during the course of thousands of experiments, but for now, let me teach you how I do my testing. A/B testing on Facebook is very much the same as you would approach any other A/B test. On Facebook, you run many different versions of a similar ad, changing one important element each time and then comparing the success of each ad in the test group. You should vary the following elements of your ad:

- The picture
- Each of the aforementioned three rules—getting people to identify with the ad, appealing to their passion, and asking them to do something

The success of an ad should be based on how much you're paying per like, a simple calculation you can make by looking at the number of new likes you acquired during each test as compared to the cost of the campaign. Of 10 ads in a test group, you might find that one cost you 10 cents per fan and another $1.50, and all you changed was the picture. These are the kinds of gems you find when you have the patience to do true A/B testing.

When you find an ad that allows you to pay 25 cents or less per like, you're in decent territory. I've found the average cost per like—the amount Facebook wants you to pay for a given like—to be about $1.15 as of early 2012. That's why I consider getting a like for a quarter pretty impressive. Of course, the value of the like to your business is what should really determine a reasonable cost per like. If you are getting likes for 50 cents but making $10 per like, that would be a great situation. But

"When you really get serious about running Facebook ads, it is kind of like gambling: the goal is to patiently wait for that one moment that makes you all your money."

if you're making very little money per like, you want to get your price-per-like as low as possible.

When you really get serious about running Facebook ads, it is kind of like gambling: the goal is to patiently wait for that one moment that makes you all your money. The "jackpot" of Facebook ads is an ad so interesting to its targeted group that people click it like crazy, and as a result, you pay only a few cents per like. I have achieved this feat roughly 150 times as of this writing, and each one feels like I hit the triple 7s. If you can manage to understand the psychology of people well enough, you can amass many times more likes than your competitors have— including potential customers and tastemakers—in a short amount of time, and for a low price.

However, even if you get one ad to "go haywire" (trying to find a good slot machine term here, bear with me), that doesn't mean your work is done. Facebook ads have a short life. The effectiveness of an ad is sure to wear off in a matter of days—sometimes even hours—and you have to go back to the drawing board. But in every successful ad, a kernel of wisdom is transferred to the ad's creator. If you can write one successful ad, I believe that you'll soon be able to write them with some consistency. I would estimate that the best ad writers could make a super-successful ad every 1 in 20 attempts. (See Chapter 8, "Dominating Facebook Ads," for a more in-depth look at this subject.)

Figure 2.9 shows two examples of viral ads created by Facebook optimizer Dennis Yu. Both attracted thousands of likes for a few pennies per fan. Let's analyze them in terms of the three rules of creating a successful Facebook ad.

Figure 2.9   *A couple of viral Facebook ads created by Facebook optimizer Dennis Yu.*

- The Scooby Doo ad accomplishes rules 1 and 3—getting people to identify with the ad and asking them to perform an action—immediately. What is not apparently clear is how it appealed to people's passion. We don't know exactly because we haven't seen the targeting for the ad, but we can assume that it was shown only to Scooby Doo lovers. Because Scooby Doo is a show that many people have fond childhood memories of, it is not too much of a stretch to assume that people who listed it as an interest on their Facebook profile are passionate about the show. Thus, it satisfies all three rules and had a good chance of being successful from the start.

- The Michael Jackson ad satisfies rules 2 and 3—appealing to a passion and asking people to perform an action—very clearly. It capitalizes on the outpouring of support for Michael Jackson that occurred shortly after his death, asking MJ fans to click "like" to read about something that would, if it were true, mesmerize them. In terms of getting people to identify with the ad, they probably could have written "Are you an MJ fan?" But the targeting was almost certainly to people who listed Michael Jackson as an interest, so they were able to get away with it.

If you or someone at your company discovers a knack for tapping into advertising psychology—and you never know unless you try—it could be used to build up a Facebook fan base and gain valuable access to tastemakers.

 Note

We will visit Facebook Ads in greater detail in Chapter 8, but you should have a good sense of the program now.

You are now aware of three methods of becoming popular on Facebook. I hope one of them appeals to your talents, because any of them could make a huge difference for your company as Facebook continues to recognize tastemakers and revolve social activity around them.

Google's Pursuit of Tastemakers

Google's interest in tastemakers is just as strong as Facebook's. Whereas Facebook aims to use your tastemakers as "spokespeople" in personalized ads, Google aims to change the order of its search results based on the preferences of your tastemakers. When Google first introduced its social search efforts in 2009—showing results from the blogs of people you were connected to through Google in a separate area of the search results page—its sense of who influenced you was nonexistent. Pretty much anyone with a Google profile and a blog appeared in the "results from your social circle" section at the bottom of the page. It is safe to say that Google's early attempts at social search were not effective. What was missing was data on how influential each of your social connections was to you.

Google's next incarnation of its social strategy removed the "social circle" section from the bottom of the page and instead integrated these socially influenced results seamlessly into the organic results (see Figure 2.10). Socially influenced results had a notation below them that indicated the reason for their presence: they were shared on Twitter, Flickr, Quora, or Google Buzz. Still, the results were not any better because the social aspect of them was irrelevant—the people mentioned in the notations, although they *were* connections of yours, were not necessarily people who *influenced* you. Thus, the power of social search was still not harnessed. Without Facebook's extensive social data, Google was unable to figure out who mattered most to you, and it certainly didn't know who mattered most to you within specific categories like food, nightlife, and travel.

Figure 2.10   *The early evolution of Google's social search—from a separate section at the bottom of the results pages to full integration of social results into the organic listings, drawing from several social networks. Today, Google's social search draws mainly from its own social network, Google+.*

In January 2011, Google began drawing social connections from public Facebook pages. However, this was not the coup it was looking for. The public pages on Facebook, which include brand and celebrity pages but not personal profiles, make up only a small fraction of the data Facebook possesses. Google was still lacking the data about your "likes" and social graph that it so badly needed in order to truly personalize its results.

In April 2011, Google introduced Google +1, which was meant to be its own Like button, aiding Google in knowing which web pages people like best. The way it works is that when you are logged into a Google account, a little button appears next to each search result that reads "+1." If you like a website, you click the +1. This sends data to Google that you like this website. There are also +1 buttons spread across the web, just like the Facebook Like button widget, allowing you to "+1" a web page you like.

As the +1 button grows in popularity, it has given Google the capability to do two things:

1. Change the order of your search results, placing sites you have +1'ed ahead of other sites.

2. Show your social connections the sites you have +1'ed, personalizing *their* search results based on your preferences. In my early field tests,

I noticed that not only do +1s from my friends influence my search results, but +1s from anyone, if occurring in a large enough quantity, can move a search result higher in the rankings. Although a +1 is not yet as powerful as a link for search engine optimization purposes, I expect +1s from certain people to hold an increasingly greater weight as Google learns to better categorize your social connections.

The boldest incarnation of Google's social strategy to date is Google+, which appeared in June 2011 and was integrated into search results as "Search Plus Your World" in January 2012. Google+, ostensibly a social network, is Google's attempt to accumulate social data from scratch. If the +1 button is a brick in Google's strategy, Google+ is an entire house. Both accomplish the same purpose—gaining information about your social preferences without having to rely on outside sources such as Facebook and Twitter.

Essentially, Google+ asks you to socialize with your Gmail contacts. The concept of tastemakers is embraced wholeheartedly by Google+, as it asks you to group your contacts into "circles," or categories, such as Family, Work Friends, Baseball Team, and Karaoke Buddies.

Although the professed reason for this grouping is its usefulness to the user (it will help keep the different aspects of your life, such as your close friends and your business connections, separate), the greater reason for Google is to get detailed information about the relative importance of each of your contacts so that it can make more sophisticated social recommendations. This means better search results, an entry ticket to the lucrative world of social discovery (see Chapter 3, "Social and Contextual Discovery"), and, the bottom line of it all: more advertising dollars.

At the time of this writing, Google still cannot place your money manager's favorite financial sites at the top of the results for finance-related searches; your travel agent's favorite review sites at the top for vacation-related searches; and other trusted people's recommendations on the first page of results, where Google believes they ought to be. But Google is surely trying.

No matter what happens with Google's social strategy, the company still has a long road ahead before social search is truly useful. Google needs to get enough social data so that it can feature websites in the search results from people we trust. Then it needs to figure out who we trust most in each major category of search and show us results that those people recommend. Google progressed toward that goal in March 2012 when it updated its privacy policy to allow it to use data from all of its products to influence our search results; the hope was that the new access to data would improve its social recommendations.

What remains to be seen is how Google will figure out how much to factor in our friends' opinions. As I mentioned earlier in the chapter, affinity will come to matter quite a bit. I may trust so-and-so, but do I trust his opinion over Google's so much that I want his recommendation on the first page of my search results? Even if I do trust this friend, where exactly in the first 10 results should his recommendation reside?

To help answer these questions, Google will turn to its oldest ability: analyzing a huge variety of sources on the Web to come up with the best data. It would like to draw all the data it needs solely from Google+; but if the service does not get enough traction, Google may re-explore its partnership with Twitter (which stopped powering Google's Realtime search product in July 2011) to get information on how much we value certain people's opinions. Twitter was the original tastemaker determiner, inventing a system where you "follow" people whose daily musings you want to hear. The people with the most followers on Twitter are powerful tastemakers and are considered thought leaders by many. Google could look at patterns of engagement on Twitter to determine who you interact with most, especially whose tweets you "retweet" (repeat to your own followers) and share on other social networks or through email. By cross-referencing email, browsing history, Google+ and +1 data, and any other data that other social networks offer, Google hopes to gain enough information on all of us to make the social search experience work.

Escalation of Tensions Around Tastemaker Data

If Google had its way, it would put a straw in the data milkshake of every popular website out there and make itself into a complete expert on what you want to see when you perform a search. Although this would give Google an unfair advantage over any search engine, current or future, it would certainly be good for the user (privacy issues aside). However, this situation cannot exist as long as a free, competitive market exists. The big websites want to protect their data so that *they* have the opportunity to personalize your experience and profit from it. And when they perceive that another company is infringing on that ability, they resort to desperate measures.

In May 2011, a fracas broke out when news hit that Facebook had secretly hired a PR firm to expose Google's alleged privacy issues in social search. The incident was said to be a response to Facebook's resentment over Google harvesting public Facebook page information. While the event underscores the bitter rivalry between the two giants, it points out one very interesting thing: Facebook's perceived weakness. Knowing that Facebook is nervous about Google's social search plans is one more in a list of reasons why I believe that, despite all its setbacks, Google will eventually get social search right—even if it's a different kind of social search than Facebook's or Bing's.

Speaking of Bing, in the same time period when Facebook revealed that it was threatened by Google's social search product, it gave ammunition to the Microsoft-owned search company to develop a more powerful social search of its own. The change that Bing announced was basically the same one that Google had announced a few months earlier—that social results were now sewn seamlessly into the organic results on Bing.com. This is true except for one big difference: Bing's social results are fueled by Facebook social data. Google, eat your heart out.

Google probably felt about Bing debuting the first legitimate social search product in history the same way that the Americans felt about Russia launching a man into space before them: pissed off. And yet, Bing's social search product completely lacks the tastemaker factor, recommending results from friends whose opinions you may not care about. Even Bing's director, in an interview with technology blog TechCrunch, admitted that the new rollout was not "the ultimate social search."

It brings me back to my earlier point about how much we, the users, would benefit if the biggest websites shared data. If Facebook shared its social data with Google, the resulting product (I'm going to keep calling it Foogle) would shed light on relationships between people in various contexts, fueling search results—and even ads—that are more relevant and interesting than ever.

Ironically, it doesn't seem like Facebook plans to do much with social search anyway. If it did, why would it allow Bing to use its precious data to create a social search of its own? Facebook's partnership with Bing speaks of a Facebook whose sights are set on something even more interesting to them: social discovery.

3

Social and Contextual Discovery

When I first set out to write this book, I assumed it would cover, among other things, the evolution of search. But as I began piecing together a vision of the way we'll use the Internet in the future, I realized our habits are changing so substantially that before too long the word "search" won't even describe what companies like Google and Microsoft (Bing) do. Typing words into a box has become outdated, and websites assume a sort of passivity on behalf of the user, a reward for all the data the user has given to search engines and social media sites in the last decade. Information retrieval is becoming information attraction. Thus, social and contextual discovery have come into being.

Social Discovery

Social discovery is the sibling to social search. By definition, it is the act of a website presenting content that is predicted to be desirable or relevant to a person based on that person's social preferences. I like to say it's an algorithm that tells you what you want before you want it.

At the center of social discovery is Facebook. By encouraging people to "like" people, brands, and content, Facebook effectively controls an army of unwitting spokespeople. Your grandma Sue's innocent mouse-click, indicating a fondness for *The Joy Of Cooking*, finds its way into an ad that reads: "Sue Smith likes *The Joy Of Cooking*," with a picture of your venerable grandmother along with an image of the cookbook and a link to its page on Facebook. Without realizing it, Grandma has become an endorser, not unlike Michael Jordan sporting a pair of Nikes (but less tall).

There are two reasons social discovery exists. The first is that it is part of the natural evolution of the Internet, which has presented us information first in human-edited directories, then in a multitude of websites and blogs, then on social bookmarking sites like Digg and de.licio.us, and most recently on social networks. Now that we have so much data on our likes, interests, and connections, both social and work-related, we are ready for the next phase of information delivery, one that is even more convenient: the delivery of personalized results through search and discovery.

The second reason social discovery exists is that it is certain to be extremely profitable for the companies that get it right. Facebook in particular needs social discovery in order to succeed as a megabusiness. Whereas Google search is overtly linked to commerce because it is the tool people use to research anything they want to buy, Facebook is a utility people use to connect with friends, and there are far fewer commercial associations with friendship. There are, however, some, and Facebook has explored a number of the natural avenues. Gaming is one of the most obvious ones, because people love to play games with their friends. Serving ads for group-buying sites like Groupon has been another good revenue driver because people love to get deals with their friends.

Transitioning Facebook from a purely personal space to a business tool, which occurred in late 2007 with the introduction of brand pages and ads, was an essential move for Facebook. As I mentioned in the previous chapter, Facebook's ad-targeting capabilities give it a true differentiator in the advertising world. However, Facebook's ultimate success will depend on the public's embrace of buying products and services they weren't looking for, that they serendipitously discovered and fell in love with.

If we break social discovery down into its most basic form, it is essentially a massive assembly of labels—or, in Internet speak, *tags*. Tags are notes that help us expand our knowledge of objects on the Web, especially objects that a computer can't fully analyze. A picture, for instance, might be tagged with a location, resolution, camera type, and a description about what is happening in the picture. Any modern camera could automatically generate all those tags except for the last one. Subjective descriptions are still well within the realm of human-only knowledge, which is why tagging exists.

In an ideal world, we would tag every picture, video, and experience we have online so social sites like Facebook could have a full description of every person, place, and thing we care about. It could then easily cross-reference people's experiences algorithmically to suggest great new content for them. Because people aren't willing to do all that work for the benefit of social networks, these sites have had to invent clever ways to get people's opinions on things. Hence the invention of likes, +1s, upvotes, diggs, and other one-click indicators of preference. The point is to make it so effortless to supply data to websites that plenty of people end up doing it.

By substituting general positive/negative votes for the detailed descriptions they would ideally like, social networks miss out on a ton of social data that would help them advance in social search and discovery; but it seems they have concluded that if they asked the public to do anything more complicated than clicking a Like button, they'd get far less data. I think that remains to be seen. After people see the new world that social data can open up for them, I believe they'll be more willing to share information. That is why sites like Quora (a high quality question and answer site), which are social but require a huge output of information from its users, work: there is a feeling of community, that by putting out good information, you will get good information in return.

> "After people see the new world that social data can open up for them, I believe they'll be more willing to share information."

Indeed, Facebook is gearing up to ask more of its users. At the same time it consistently pushes users to accept a less and less private environment, it requests more data from them. If you think back a bit, you'll see what I mean. A few years ago, Facebook just required you to fill out a profile and add photos. Then suddenly it asked you to "tag" your friends, which felt like a bit of work at first. Next, it asked you to indicate all your interests using the Like button. Soon Facebook will be asking you to tag again, but this time it will want you to tag products. In May 2011, the first glimpse of this next phase of knowledge transfer occurred when Facebook announced the capability to tag your pictures with the names of brand and celebrity pages.

I believe that Facebook will eventually decide that it has habituated its users to sharing data well enough that it can begin getting more information from the start. While writing this book, I predicted that Facebook would start asking you to categorize your social connections the moment you add them as friends. In September 2011, they began doing so, offering you just "close friend" and "acquaintance" as options. I predict these categories will become more granular in time: perhaps "family member," "close friend," "acquaintance," and "business connection." I believe most people will go ahead and categorize their social connections. After all, doing so feels like filling out a personal questionnaire, which is fun. Figure 3.1 shows an example of what this might look like.

Facebook may even go a step further and ask you to rate how much you value each new friend's opinion. If we aren't comfortable sharing that information today, we will be a year or two from now. This is how Facebook will eventually learn who tastemakers are and enable social discovery to be more useful. In the coming months and years, expect to see continued movement toward social discovery and the commercialization of your social life.

Figure 3.1   *A possible way Facebook will collect more information about the affinity of each of your friends so it can better deliver personalized data.*

How Facebook Will Incorporate New Types of Social Advertising

Allow me to describe the landscape that marketers will soon be playing on. I expect the following five features to be incorporated into Facebook soon.

- Richer tagging
- New, purchase-related "stories" in the News Feed
- Better information on friends and their activities
- More personalized deals
- Birthday gift suggestions

Richer Tagging

The capability to tag businesses, brands, and public figures in photos is vital to Facebook's evolving social advertising vision, because it allows Facebook to see which brands people interact with most. After it has data on the brands people tag most, Facebook can ask those brands for advertising money whenever they appear in photos. It won't be long before all types of products, places, and even services are taggable. In the future, as people browse through each other's pictures (which is currently the most popular action on Facebook), they will be able to buy the products, services, or experiences they see.

Let's look at three examples of the ways these new tags will be used.

Example #1: A Product

Figure 3.2 shows a mock-up in which the sneakers worn by my fiancée and me are tagged and can be purchased on Facebook.

Figure 3.2 *This vacation photo could end up selling shoes on Facebook.*

Example #2: A Service

The mock-up in Figure 3.3 shows a horseback riding tour company that is tagged, and anyone who sees my picture has the opportunity to book the same trip from the company I used.

Figure 3.3   *Want to book the same trip I went on? Click the photo and you can.*

Example #3: A Place or Experience

The mock-up in Figure 3.4 shows me at a rock concert. The concert venue is tagged, as is the artist, and both businesses are advertised.

Figure 3.4   *Want to see this artist when he tours near you, or see another show at the same venue? Click the photo.*

This innovation in ads will be the best social advertising product on the market because it targets the excitement of interacting with a friend's picture, and happens to do so on the most popular photo-sharing site on Earth. However, affinity will be a crucial factor here; if I am a tastemaker to some of my friends, they are far more likely to want to purchase something I have purchased than if I am not influential to them. If Facebook can nail the affinity factor, it will give Google's ad product, Adwords, a run for its money. Not only would succeeding in social discovery be profitable, it would open up a whole new chapter in advertising. It would prove that you can generate interest in products when people aren't looking for them and aren't physically in front of them. After all, everyone knows you can persuade a person who is walking through Walmart to buy a set of knives if you wow them by cutting through a brick, but getting the same person to buy those knives simply by showing them a picture of friends using the knives is far quicker and more scalable.

> "If Facebook can nail the affinity factor, it will give Google's ad product, Adwords, a run for its money."

New, Purchase-Related "Stories" in the News Feed

Facebook knows that if it can find a way to add value to its users' experience by updating them about their friends' purchases, it stands to gain a great new referral model. Currently, the News Feed tells you what your friends like once in a while—such as, "Janice Cho likes Gilmore Girls." But if it also told you what your friends purchased, the concept would be taken a step further. Anyone can like something, but would they *buy* it? It is possible this extra psychological nudge would trigger more ad clicks and dollars spent.

I think people would be very interested in what their friends spend money on. I can picture seeing stories like "Anna bought a Toyota Prius" and "Randy went to The Boom Boom Room" popping up, and I would enjoy reading about it as a kind of vicarious peek into people's lives. If the success of Foursquare and Facebook Places is any indicator, people love getting gossip about real-life things their friends have done.

One of the more interesting startups that is already allowing us to examine our friends' purchases is Blippy.com. Blippy integrates with your credit card company and announces every purchase you make to your social circle. The purpose is to allow friends to see what you buy so they can potentially buy the same things, and to generate conversation among people who have purchased the same items. Ashvin Kumar, Blippy's CEO, told me that he knows Blippy will take some time to go mainstream, because it asks users to change their online behavior. "In the same way that Amazon changed the way people shop, Facebook changed the way people socialize, and Groupon changed the way people get local deals, Blippy will change the way people interact with their personal finances by making it into a social experience." I think that Blippy is interesting because, as a company backed by some of the biggest venture capitalists in Silicon Valley, it represents a deep belief in the power of your social circle to influence purchases. It, along with a number of other startups whose names you don't know yet, forms the foundation of a future where the packaging of data about other people's lives makes you a more informed—and active—consumer than ever before.

Better Information on Friends and their Activities

At the 2011 F8 Developers Conference, Mark Zuckerberg made a few key annnouncements. Except for some design changes, all of the announcements amounted to Facebook's attempt to capture more data in order to richen their offering to advertisers. The new profile contained a timeline feature, which encouraged users to input information about themselves from the past, dating back to when they were born. And the new social buttons, called "gestures," essentially meant that the Like button was to become the antecedent of a long line of verbs you can use to tell your friends about what you're doing. Giving users the ability to express actions beyond simple approval (for isn't that what "like" basically means?) allows advertisers to understand users' views on their products much better. For instance, it is more powerful for a movie studio to know that 230,000 people watched a movie rather than just liked it. And it is more powerful for a political campaign to know that 150,000 people cheered their cause rather than just liked it.

More Personalized Deals

Facebook knows precisely how important deals are (as does Google, who tried to purchase Groupon but got rebuffed). Think of the success that Groupon, Living Social, and all the clones out there have had by offering deals that aren't overly personalized; if only they knew as much about you as Facebook does! Truly, Facebook has the capability to customize offers and deals to you like no other. And it will capitalize on that as soon as a critical mass of advertisers begin participating in deal-related advertising.

Birthday Gift Suggestions

How difficult would it be for Facebook to offer a list of suggested gifts for someone a week before his or her birthday? And how welcome and useful? Finding the right gift for a friend is an age-old problem that is ripe to be solved by a website that knows what you like. More social data will be needed before Facebook can truly do justice to this idea—but Facebook will have it soon.

Facebook can grow its data set only through your participation, so expect to see more encouragement to "gesture" ("like" and all the other verbs), comment, answer questions, and generally interact with friends online. As the number of connections between people, places, and products becomes greater—and the social graph becomes richer as a result—Facebook will tie up that huge net and fill it with money. If you are a tastemaker to your friends, you will probably be pestered more than most to tag your pictures, participate in deals, announce your plans and purchases, and generally function more like a commercial user. In fact, I wouldn't be surprised if there was some internal debate within Facebook about whether to share money with tastemakers. Although it is a risky proposition to turn friends into salesmen, it could make sense for some people, especially public figures. If Facebook can get friends interested in selling products to their friends—actively or passively—it will have created the ultimate referral machine.

> "If Facebook can get friends interested in selling products to their friends—actively or passively—it will have created the ultimate referral machine."

Thus is the path to world domination for Facebook—and a far more personalized experience for you. The trick will be maintaining an environment that feels increasingly more social and interesting without letting monetization become too obvious. If people feel like a wallet, they will abandon ship. But if Facebook can add value to users' lives through social discovery *while* making money, it will have struck the perfect balance.

Contextual Discovery

Contextual discovery, a concept I first heard about through Google spokesperson Marissa Mayer at a developers' conference in late 2010, is like social discovery but personalizes content based on *where* you are rather than *who* you are. So, let's say you're at the airport. A notification may pop up on your mobile phone telling you your flight's status, as well as showing you a map of the airport. As with Facebook's evolving social discovery product, there is a tension between providing value for the user and the temptation to capitalize on the user's attention through advertising. And so, alongside the notifications that help you through your flight experience, you will probably be informed of a deal at the airport Starbucks or a discount on in-flight Wi-Fi.

More so than Facebook, I trust Google to keep the usefulness factor top-of-mind while downplaying the ads. Google has a history of making our lives easier, and the trade-off—having to look at little text ads alongside the experience—hasn't been that bad. Compare text ads to the annoyingness of a pop-up ad or a pre-roll video commercial and you'll see what I mean.

Contextual discovery is not a product that just any company can offer. In its mobile form, it either needs to be sewn into your phone by the software maker or be part of a location-based application. To deliver

> "Google has a history of making our lives easier, and the trade-off—having to look at little text ads alongside the experience—hasn't been that bad."

contextual information, a company must not only know where you are and what you're doing, but also have information to share with you about every place and activity. To do so, it would need a large bank of local data and a preestablished group of advertisers. Google is a natural fit. It seems likely it had contextual discovery in mind when it decided to create Android, its mobile phone operating system. Other natural fits are Foursquare and Gowalla, who have always based their business models on being able to serve you relevant ads wherever you are.

As with mobile payments, the company that can get you to remain logged in all the time has the competitive advantage. Whoever is always present in the background can easily add to your experience by offering information based on where you are and what you're doing. Google remains the strongest contender, based on this reasoning, with its nearly 200 million worldwide users (as of this printing); the majority of them are logged in 24/7. Although Facebook's users also tend to stay logged in, and there are three times as many, its core product is so social that it is unlikely Facebook would deliver purely utilitarian content like maps, menus, and guides. Truly, contextual discovery is meant to be offered by Google, whose mission is to make the world's information "universally accessible and useful."

In fact, I would call Google the original inventor of contextual discovery. Its AdSense ads, which "read" web pages and serve you ads that relate to the content on the page, were the first of their kind. I believe Google will continue to innovate in this area with its Chrome web browser (see Figures 3.5 and 3.6). After all, contextual discovery doesn't have to be mobile; it can also be in the browser. Soon we will be seeing notifications pop up while we're surfing the Web. If you are searching for a used car, for instance, your Chrome web browser might offer you a copy of the current year's Blue Book, which lists the values of used cars. Some of the content Chrome offers will simply be helpful and interesting, with no advertising basis. But ads will always be a part of the experience in some form.

Figure 3.5 *A likely application of Google's contextual discovery, which Google calls "Google search without the search." Here, the user is being offered a peek at the menu while he is browsing the restaurant's website.*

Figure 3.6 *Another likely application of contextual discovery. This web browser offers reviews of the book the person is viewing.*

Google bills contextual discovery as "Google search without the search," and it will undoubtedly be an important part of the company's future. I can imagine it applying to travel guides, TV programming, cooking recipes, reviews, and much more. As a predominantly mobile service, I can picture it expanding to useful suggestions about other parts of your phone, as well. For instance, because I live on both coasts, it would be useful if my phone "knew" that upon landing in New York, I usually want to call a taxi; and that in the taxi, I often call one of three or four people to let them know I'll be home in a little while. Then, at home, I like to "check in" through Facebook to announce to my New York friends that I'm back. With contextual discovery, all these actions could be offered to me instantly, and I could accomplish each one in a single click!

As you can see, there is a lot of potential in contextual discovery—but how can it be useful to marketers?

Capitalizing on Contextual Discovery

Because contextual discovery is all about providing useful content to users, a marketer who wants to capitalize on it will need to create such content. Doing so fits nicely into the most effective philosophy for both SEO and social media: "Content is king." That's an old adage, but it has become more true than ever with the rise of social media and Google's recent algorithm updates. When you have a landscape where the dominant search engine is focused on promoting valuable websites, and the dominant social media site is focused on people recommending valuable websites, there is pretty much no choice but to put your time and energy into creating something...well, valuable.

To give you an example of a website that is truly useful to people, look back at Figure 3.5, where Google's Chrome browser offers a menu to its user while the user is looking at a restaurant site. The winner in that equation is the site that is offering the menu. They are getting a traffic boost from Google's referencing their site. Why? Because they provide something with real value—an informational aid. If your site is a high-quality review site, news site, guide, or anything else in the category of a "resource," it has the chance to be used by Google in its contextual discovery product.

Because most resources generally don't make money, I do not advocate creating a superb guide to such-and-such solely to receive a traffic boost. The correct course of action is to make your site, which sells products or services of some kind, into the authority in its niche. *Supplement* what you sell with a resources section, and place ads on all the pages in that section that lead people back to the place where they can make a purchase. For instance, suppose you sell flowers. Apart from your main product pages, which show pictures of the types of flowers you sell, have a Flower Guide, and spend a while making it one of the best resources about flowers out there, with crisp pictures, detailed descriptions, and other fun extras. The last part is the most important. If you simply list hundreds of flower types and write a sentence about each one, people would have no reason to come to your site; they could go to Wikipedia instead (which, by the way, will be the ultimate recipient of traffic from contextual discovery for obvious reasons). But let's say you included on the page for each flower a special section that describes the occasion each flower type works for best. Maybe daisies are great for graduations and daffodils are best to say you're sorry. Who knows? *You* do, if you make a guide. And if Google sees sites linking to it and people +1ing (i.e. "liking") it, it will be used by contextual discovery and bring your site a windfall of traffic.

Because contextual discovery is closer to local and mobile search than it is to web search or social media, the companies that should care most about optimizing for it are the ones who serve local economies or aggregate local information. TripAdvisor, Fodors, Yelp, and Zagat are the most prominent examples in the space. If your company serves a local market or is intended to be viewed on mobile phones, you should care about contextual discovery.

And, at the risk of repeating myself, like social discovery, contextual discovery will rely on people's recommendations. If you hear from people that they love the information provided on your company's website or app, you will be positioning yourself to get new business from many different sources.

4

Real-Time Search and the Culture of Status Updates

If you told a person living in the year 2001 that, within a decade, there would be trillions of one-line updates about what people are doing at a given moment, he would probably ask, "Why?" And if you challenged this same person to come up with a use for all that information, he'd likely stumble. It is counterintuitive to think that people's random thoughts matter much. But the Internet works in funny ways. It ended up proving that, if you get enough random thoughts and make them searchable, you can discover patterns among the public that shine light on human behavior.

From a marketing perspective, real-time search, the interface through which we sort through this mountain of information using keywords and topic indicators, is golden. It has given us a way to understand and quantify people's opinions in huge numbers. On the other hand, it has also given us a way to connect with individuals we may never have met otherwise. In many ways, it was the first manifestation of social search, a method of finding news and opinion that straddled personal interaction and impersonal research.

The uses of real-time search are many. Let's say you're in medical school and are trying to decide which field to specialize in. Apart from the field that most interests you, it would be useful to get a sense of which one is more in demand than others, as well as the common situations you would face as a specialist. Real-time search could give you insight. Try typing "toe" or "my foot" into the search box, and you will see thousands of updates where people talk about their toes and feet. Compare the quantity of search results to, say, a search for "my spine," and you could glean the relative size of podiatry versus spinal orthopedics. Then, having found that podiatry is a much larger field, you could browse through the common things people complain about. "The soles of my feet hurt when I walk"; "My big toe has a shooting pain in it," and other such updates would give you a sense of the situations you'd encounter in the words of the average person.

Or, suppose you are starting a kitchen remodeling business. Knowing which kinds of tile to stock may be easy enough, but anticipating what problems people encounter with each kind of tile might be very useful. Inputting "ceramic tile broken" or "porcelain tile broken" would give you some insights into people discussing their specific type of broken tile. Very few sources could offer such specificity so quickly.

In no particular order, here are a few more applications of real-time search:

- A movie producer could search for various actors' names to measure public opinion about each one in order to aid him in casting an upcoming movie.
- A web design company could search for specific blogging and content management systems to hear users' honest opinions about each one and decide which to recommend for clients' websites.
- A fashion designer could search the names of different styles of jeans in order to get a sense of what people like and dislike about each style.
- A freelance writer could look through recently trending topics on a real-time search engine to find a hot subject for his next story.

I hope at this point you are thinking about your own business or organization and how real-time search could be useful for it. I have yet to find an industry that can't benefit from it.

Real-Time Search's Homes

So where on the Internet can you find real-time search? Twitter, the pioneer of status updates, is the main source. This is due mostly to its popularity and public nature. In contrast to Facebook, which has the feel of a private social network, Twitter is meant to be a place where anyone can read what you write, or "tweet." Twitter.com/search was the original place to perform real-time search and is still a great tool; however, data usage issues have caused Twitter to hide tweets that are more than 10 days old, so if you are looking for a historical record of status updates—for example, to study the way people have reacted to a certain product or person for the past two years—you won't have an easy time doing it on Twitter. For that kind of research, you would turn to one of the several real-time search engines that feed off of Twitter's data pipes, such as Topsy.com.

Twitter Search's advanced features are pretty much the only reason to use it instead of one of the third party real-time search engines. You can find the features by clicking the Advanced Search link below the search box and then searching for "positive" tweets, "negative" tweets, and questions (see Figure 4.1). The smaller sites' advantages are more numerous, however. They include the capability to search through all historical status updates from Twitter, find experts on a particular topic, find out the public's sentiment on any subject, and search through photographs in real time.

Figure 4.1   *A search on twitter.com/realtime for "mitt romney" that is filtered to show only status updates that have negative feelings in them. Although the positive/negative filter isn't always accurate, it gives a taste of the ways real-time search can be used to measure public sentiment.*

Figure 4.2 *A Google realtime search for "Adele" filtered by the time period "June 2011" gives us a snapshot of the public's opinion in June 2011 of the singer.*

It would only make sense for the king of search, Google, to have a real-time search engine. Of course, status updates are necessary to create such a product. That was the snag that Google ran into when it first made plans to create Google.com/realtime, which debuted in 2009 and took a hiatus in July 2011. The search engine relied almost completely on Twitter status updates, with a small slice derived from Facebook's public pages, Google Buzz, Google News, and other sources such as LinkedIn, MySpace, Flickr, and Quora. Relying on another company's data to support a major up-and-coming function of your search engine is a precarious idea, and alas, despite Google.com/realtime's many strengths, it came crashing down when Google and Twitter failed to renew their partnership. Sources within Google told me that it was Twitter that ultimately walked away, most likely deciding that the traffic it received from Google wasn't worth handing over its entire library of tweets so that Google could do real-time search better than Twitter does.

In Google's perfect world, it would have access to all tweets and Facebook status updates, allowing the search giant to do what it does best—parse

> "In Google's perfect world, it would have access to all tweets and Facebook status updates, allowing the search giant to do what it does best—parse through mountains of information and come up with only the best results."

through mountains of information and come up with only the best results. Alas, the competition between search companies and social networks is too fierce at this stage in the game. This reality is what pushed Google to make a huge bet on Google+: It realized it needed its own social data or else real-time search, and many other initiatives, would be dead on arrival.

The June 2011 disappearance of Google Realtime search was a huge opportunity for Bing, which has the utopia that Google is looking for in its access to all public Facebook status updates, as well as Twitter status updates. However, Bing has not taken advantage of this gift, keeping its real-time search so limited as to be almost useless. It is beyond me why Bing doesn't add more features to its real-time search, which is currently the same as Twitter's search, except that duplicates, spam, and adult content have been filtered out. Although real-time search is not the revenue opportunity that social search and social discovery are, it is still an opportunity to excel in an area of search that is emerging quickly—and one in which Bing has a rare advantage.

Whoever takes the initiative to really blow out real-time search's capabilities will capture the imagination of the searcher. Picture, if you will, a real-time search engine that is filtered not just by time, location, and association with an image, but also by gender, age, profession, education, interest, political affiliation, mood, and commerciality—just to name a few.

As marketers, we should be eagerly hoping for a sense of competition to spark in the real-time search arena so that Google, Bing, Twitter, and Facebook start trying to outdo each other. When the options I just described are finally included in a real-time search interface—and I dare say it won't be too hard to do, especially if the implementation isn't perfect—we'll be able to observe the Internet in a brand new way. We'll be able to search for status updates from 36–45-year-old American women who play online games (see Figure 4.3), or musings from British business owners about the economy, or thoughts from left-wing political pundits in November 2012. The quality of research we'll be able to do will be dramatically better than it is today.

Figure 4.3 *A mock real-time search interface showing a query for game-related posts from women 36–45 years old who live in the United States. Marketers for online game companies would love insights from this valuable demographic. This is one of many potential applications of real-time search done to its full potential.*

Profiting from Real-Time Search: The Search and Sell Method

Embedded in all uses of real-time search, as in every marketing activity, is the goal of making money. Real-time search is an excellent way to ascertain leads, one by one, using targeted searches. All that is involved in doing so is coming up with a creative search that will yield potential customers for your business and then messaging those people in a casual way to propose your services. In the last chapter of my first book, *Outsmarting Google*, I gave the example of a wedding invitation designer using real-time search to find new clients by typing "I'm engaged" into the search box and then offering his wedding invitation services to every person who announced their engagement that day. I can attest to the fact that this method works, having done it for clients of widely differing professions. The oddest was probably the gynecologist for whom I located women who publicly announced that they were experiencing discomfort. I drew the line at the personal injury lawyer who asked me to find him victims of traffic accidents. Indeed, real-time search is a versatile marketing tool.

Figure 4.4 shows an example of a search actually performed by a client who sells luggage that is made to be especially convenient for going through airport security. By searching for people's gripes about airport security, he found hundreds of new potential customers to communicate with.

Figure 4.4   *A real-time search result that a company who sells "airport-friendly" luggage could use to find new customers. Searching "airport security," the company is trying to identify people complaining about airport security so they can direct them to the luggage website. As it turns out, two of the six users shown here (indicated with arrows) seem like promising leads.*

The following sections provide a step-by-step guide to the "search and sell" method, as I like to call it.

Devise Clever Search Phrases that Return Status Updates From Potential Customers

This is a bit of a creative project. Put yourself in the mind of persons in your target audience: what might they say in a status update? Let's say you sell cell phones. People who are looking to buy a new cell phone will probably be in one of three situations. Either they are replacing their current cell phone because they want a newer phone; they are replacing their current cell phone because it's broken; or they have never had a cell phone. The last one is so unlikely that we can just eliminate it. (However, as an exercise in creative thinking, it's good to think of all situations your potential customers could be in.) Of the two remaining situations, the broken cell phone jumps out at me. Someone with a broken cell phone is likely to announce it to their friends online so that they know why the person isn't responding to texts or calls, and to encourage them to communicate through Facebook, Twitter, or email instead. Therefore, the situation is ripe for the picking. Search "cell phone broken," "cell phone died," "cell phone dead," or "cell phone lost," and you probably have a huge pool of customers right there. The other situation, where people want to update their cell phone, has a less-elegant solution, but a solution nonetheless. This group of potential customers might be seeking advice about which cell phone to buy, and a social network like Facebook or Twitter is an ideal place to procure such advice. A search for "which cell phone" is likely to yield some people in the market for a new cell phone.

Inherent in this kind of guesswork is an understanding of the way people use status updates. If you update your status on a social network frequently, this point may be fairly obvious to you, but if not, keep the following rule in mind: People update their status to tell their online friends what they are doing or thinking about, or to ask a question. Status updates range from the simple report ("Reading Calvin and Hobbes") to the random musing ("I wonder how often they change the cocktail nuts at bars.") to the rant ("I can't believe Great Britain was passed over for the Olympics AGAIN!") to the momentous announcement ("Two more days until I marry the love of my life!"). When they're questions, they are usually surveylike in nature, an attempt to poll the crowd ("Who saw that Doritos commercial at halftime?").

Identify the Usernames of Your Target Customers

Typically, whatever query you type into a real-time search box is going to deliver you some good leads and some irrelevant ones. In the "cell phone lost" example, for instance, many status updates may be complaints about cell phones that lost reception rather than announcements that the person has lost a cell phone. Take note of the usernames of the good leads and skip over the bad. You should "follow" anyone that is a prime candidate to become a customer of your business. This will help you to keep track of all the people you'd like to message. If your followings ever become too hard to keep track of, you always have the option of unfollowing people later on.

 Note

When I talk about "following" people, I am using the language of Twitter. Whether you are using real-time search through Google, Bing, or one of the smaller sites, the majority of their results will be Twitter status updates ("tweets"). You may choose to use Twitter search directly so that you can easily follow your potential customers rather than having to copy their usernames into Twitter later on.

Take Your Time Contacting Leads

Before reaching out to anyone, you must be an active member of whatever social network the lead you are contacting is posting from. Again, because Twitter is the largest source of public status updates, you will likely have to sign up for Twitter. If you are a marketer or business owner, you are probably familiar with Twitter already. The only reasonable way to contact someone through Twitter is through a 140-character "at message," which simply means that you type an @ symbol followed by the person's username into the update box and then begin your message. For example, my username on Twitter is "ineffable111," so if you want to contact me, you can go to the main update box and type "@ineffable111 Hey I'm reading your book right now." (Try it now; I'd love to say hi to you.) At messages are also known as "mentions" because they are often used when you are tweeting about someone and want the person to know you have acknowledged them. For example, as you can see in Figure 4.5, you could write a tweet containing "@ineffable111" and I would see it and have the option of replying to your @ message.

inter
mark
nstit @mktginstitute
Mary O'Brien

@ineffable111 Lovely to meet you last night. I enjoyed our conversation. Looking forward to chatting today and reading your book :)

23 May via web

☆ Favorite   ♺ Retweet   ↩ Reply

Figure 4.5   *An @ message, also known as a "mention." This is the best way to contact someone on Twitter.*

When you are contacting people on Twitter for commercial purposes, there are a couple of ground rules to keep in mind. The most important is that your account cannot appear to exist purely for marketing reasons or people will be instantly turned off. People can see all your @ messages, and if they are simply a series of commercial requests, you will not just be ignored but reported as a spammer. Instead, I advise sending no more than 5–7 commercial @ messages per day, interspersing them with real updates about what you're doing, thinking about, or reading online. If you update more than 10 times per day, you risk being annoying to anyone who has chosen to follow you, which, for the purposes of the search and sell method, is a bad idea because it hinders the "sell" part of the equation.

When it comes to approaching people, the best way to succeed is to come across as a legitimate, likeable person. As with any cold sales pitch, you essentially have only one chance to catch someone's interest. When I reach out to people on Twitter, the fact that I have tens of thousands of followers but follow only a few people helps me because it suggests that I am a person who is worth "following." But even in my case, when I @ message people who don't know me, my response rate is only about 1 in 5. It would be considerably lower if I had fewer followers, no matter how effective my actual message was. That's OK though; I am only telling you this so you can set your expectations low.

When you @ message someone, there is a good likelihood that the recipient will check you out. Twitter reveals your bio, picture, follower statistics, and latest tweets when someone clicks your username, so you should curate that information carefully before embarking on a search and sell. Your picture should be of you, not a logo, and should be warm and sincere looking. Your bio should be "spun" in the most interesting way possible, while remaining simple and down to earth. To give you a sense of what I mean, let's take a theoretical company that sells watches.

A GOOD TWITTER BIO:

> Since 1928, the Borecci family has been passionately crafting time-pieces by hand. Our legacy is defined by our attention to detail and lifetime service guarantee for all customers. http://www.borecci.com

A BAD TWITTER BIO:

> Are you looking for a truly unique watch? Look no further. Borecci watches come with a lifetime service guarantee. These extremely elegant timepieces will last for generations. http://www.borecci.com

The basic difference between the two bios is that the first one feels straightforward, inspired, and carefully written, whereas the second one feels like a familiar sales pitch.

If you want to be received well by potential customers, it's also a good idea to spend some time building up your numbers, especially your followers. The easiest way to do that is to follow people. Most people who are not celebrities will follow you back. Because you don't want the number of people you follow to be higher than the number of followers you have, you should unfollow most people who don't follow you back. Of course, feel free to follow people whose tweets you genuinely want to see, whether or not they follow you

"When you have at least 100 followers, you are legitimate; 500 and you look like an active user; and with 1,000+ you come across as a very active Twitter user."

back. But for everyone else, the relationship must be reciprocal. When you have at least 100 followers, you are legitimate; 500 and you look like an active user; and with 1,000+ you come across as a very active Twitter user.

After people look at your picture, your bio, and your follower/following numbers, they will probably glance at your recent tweets. To make sure you come across as a person worth knowing, your best bet is to maintain Twitter relationships in earnest. Doing so will show that you participate in the community and that people care about what you say. Even a small number of interactions—other people mentioning you, mostly—is enough to pass most people's sniff test.

Now to the hardest part of the strategy: the message itself. The language you use is crucial. No matter what industry you're in, you should begin by anticipating the needs of the person you're messaging—whether express or implied. In the "which cell phone" search, for instance, we might find some clues about the needs of the users in these search results inside the status updates themselves. If, for instance, someone's status update reads "which cell phone company has the best service?" you know immediately what that person needs in a cell phone: good service. Therefore, an effective @ message might read:

> Blue Mobile has the best service by far—fewer dropped calls than other networks. Great prices on BM phones here: http://myshop.com

To further fine-tune your message, it is also important to visit the profile of the person you're messaging. Based on the person's picture, bio, and stream of tweets, you can probably learn about—or at least guess at—other needs. If the person who is seeking good cell phone service is 18 years old, he or she is likely to use texting a lot, and so your @ message could mention a deal for unlimited texting. In contrast, if the person seems knowledgeable in tech and lives in New York, it might make sense to take a slightly different angle, saying something like:

> Blue Mobile has lowest dropped calls of any provider and an incredible 3G network. NYC coverage is flawless. Check out http://myshop.com

Now, you may be wondering if I really expect you to research and contact every customer one by one. Isn't that too much work? The answer is, it depends on what stage you're at in your business. This kind of direct, simple sales messaging can be painstaking, but it works. The fewer customers you already have, and the more expensive your product or service is, the better the search and sell is. In other words, it is good for new businesses because it creates real, one-on-one relationships with customers and gives you a great opportunity for feedback and to create loyal advocates for your brand; separately, no matter how old your business is, if you sell a product that is expensive—for example, more than $1,000—it is also a good method because your business probably relies on relatively few purchases but a higher quality of customer interaction.

The other important thing to note about this method is that Twitter is, by nature, a social network, not a place people go to seek out purchases. For that reason, when you *are* marketing on it, you have to go really soft on the sell. In an ideal world, it would be best to start every new interaction with a discussion of the other person's interests, and then find your way naturally into a selling position. For instance, every now and then you could mention "If you ever need such-and-such, I'm your guy (or gal)." The idea is, if you strike up conversations only with people who need what you sell, eventually some of them are going to try you out.

Real-Time Search as an Advertising Aid

An indirect way to make money from real-time search is to use it to learn people's sentiments about a particular product or service and then advertise based on what you learned. If you own a startup that simplifies traffic measurement on websites, for example, you might tap into real-time search to see what people are saying about various analytics programs, or about analytics itself. Let's say you begin by searching for "google analytics." You might come across a common complaint, which is that Google Analytics undercounts traffic. If the complaint was widespread enough, it would give you fuel to base an ad campaign around the fact that your startup can help give accurate traffic measurements. The ad, which could run through Google Adwords, Facebook, or a display network, could look something like this:

Tired of your traffic being undercounted by Google?

> Analyzerpro.com simplifies analytics, giving you the most accurate traffic measurement on the web.

If the search and sell strategy exemplifies the micro-level uses of real-time search, the data-collection method embodies its macro-level uses. Real-time search data can also be used at the macro level to inform your company about what its customers are saying about it. Most businesses have commentary about them floating around on social networks. Communicating with your most vocal customers can help retain them and control public opinion about your company to some degree, which makes you money by ensuring that more money doesn't need to be spent on customer acquisition and PR.

Preparing for Real-Time 2.0

Despite all the exciting possibilities of real-time search, it sometimes seems like the clearest conclusion it has allowed us to reach in the past few years is that people love Justin Bieber. I'm half-joking, but it is true that most people use real-time search for two things: celebrity updates and news. Without celebrities, Twitter would probably be a niche service that few people had ever heard of. And usage hit a fever pitch in early 2011 during the Egyptian revolution, which was famed for being fueled by status updates on the site. The ubiquity and instantaneousness of status updates make them a powerful force in our world. But apart from news and entertainment (which often seem indistinguishable), what practical use do they have for the average person? How will real-time search evolve to stay relevant?

> "Despite all the exciting possibilities of real-time search, it sometimes seems like the clearest conclusion it has allowed us to reach in the past few years is that people love Justin Bieber."

Real-time search 2.0 is gathering momentum as we speak. It will arrive when status updates are even more popular than they are today, when a sizable portion of the population is updating their status a few times per day. Until a more meaningful data set is built, we won't have the information we need in order to know what's happening in the world on a truly granular level—especially in local places.

The following are some of the manifestations of status updates you can expect to see before too long. Most of them would work best in the form of a mobile phone app:

- **Wait time updater**—Imagine if every hour a few people in line for Space Mountain at Disneyworld typed an update on the wait time for the attraction into a special mobile app? Not only would we know when to avoid Tomorrowland, but after a while, the data could be plotted along a yearly graph so we could schedule our entire trip based on the days and times when the wait is less menacing.

- **Parking space finder**—The combination of highly accurate geolocation features on cell phones—which can detect where you are within a few feet—and real-time status update feeds could, one day, solve the parking spot problem. I can imagine an app that has one simple button, "Find Parking Spot," which, when pushed, searches your immediate vicinity for spots that have been reported as open. In exchange for the convenience the service offers, all that would be required is to push a second button when you're leaving: "Report Open Parking Space," which would record your location and add it to the database for the next person looking for parking in your area.

- **Hot spot locator**—"What's the best place to go out tonight?" is an age-old question asked by young people the world over. As many companies have tried to accurately tackle the local scene, none have succeeded in announcing which bars, clubs, restaurants, and lounges are truly rockin' at a given moment. It certainly wouldn't seem difficult for people who are already out, who are already on their cell phones constantly, to open an app that automatically detects their location and cross-references it with the name of the place they're at, and then asks them to rate the hotness of the venue on a scale from 1 to 10 and give a short comment about it. Some possible updates: "5—mostly dudes but a few cuties coming in and out." "10—Amazing music and Justin Timberlake just walked in."

- **Political pulse detector**—Although you can get a sense of the public opinion today by searching status updates on Twitter for the name of election candidates, there is not yet enough volume to get an accurate feel for the issues people care most about or who might win. Even after the volume is there, a filter will be needed that crunches the numbers and can give you more information than a Gallup poll: who is most favored and by how much, which issue each candidate is strongest and weakest on, and what the perceived successes and failures of the candidate's campaign have been, to name a few. This would probably work best as a website.

- **Yard sale alerter**—In these tough economic times, who wouldn't mind passing through a yard sale? Hey, the quality of merchandise is no worse than Craigslist: it comes from the same source. If a few of the people who noticed a garage sale poster on a local telephone poll wrote a status update about it on a mobile app, we would never have a day without knowing the location of a new garage sale. And from there, who knows? Maybe we would help build our local economy, spend less and trade more, and meet all our neighbors.

Benefiting from Real-Time 2.0

When these kinds of real-time–reliant services materialize, there will be one hard-and-fast rule: *The one who updates the most, rules.* Each one of the previous examples could be taken advantage of by someone who does a lot of status updating. The owner of a bar could update about the awesomeness of his bar on the Hot Spot

Locator app many times, artificially pumping up his venue's visibility. A person with a lot of stuff to sell could post a new yard sale a few times per

"The one who updates the most, rules."

day on the Yard Sale Locator app, making her house into a veritable eBay. Yes, the creators of these real-time apps could put spam rules into place, but there is not much one can do in the face of a determined, status-updating fiend—especially one who has read this book.

Keep in mind, however, that the goal is to make the world aware of your brand without telling them about it so many times that they feel antipathy toward your brand instead. Think about Craigslist for a moment. When you are browsing through furniture listings, if you see two separate posts about the same piece of furniture, you don't think too much about it; you just pass the second one by. But if you see 10 posts about the same piece of furniture and it is hindering your ability to browse through the listings, you begin to get annoyed. Don't be that annoying guy.

Instead—and I believe this is the key to success on all social sites at the present time—try to build a passionate group of advocates. Let them do the status updating for you. By doing so right now, while real-time search (and social media in general) is still a Wild West, you will be sowing the seeds of future success.

In real-time 2.0, people are important. Your friends, business network, followers, and fans are the ones who will make sure new business keeps coming in. It's word of mouth embedded into an algorithm. As status updates begin to reflect the public's opinion on a larger scale, the voices of the people who comment on your company publicly will be louder than ever. And so, building a base of even a few dozen people who consistently talk about your company on social media sites will pay off tremendously. Most businesses do not have such a group of loyal supporters, and it's purely because they haven't made it a goal.

When thinking about the types of advocates you'd like to attract, look for two key characteristics: influence and energy. The best advocate is well-respected by many and actively excited about your brand. This combination is rare, but finding either characteristic in a supporter is valuable. I have already talked at length about the importance of influential people (tastemakers) in your social network. Energetic supporters are another form of tastemaker and are just as valuable. I would take, for instance, a regular joe who was bubbling over with enthusiasm for my company over a mega-influential person who didn't care that much about my company any day. It's kind of like assembling a board of directors. Would you rather have Bill Gates technically lend his name to your board but never show up at any meetings or talk about your company, or a very popular local schoolteacher who fervently tells everyone she meets that they absolutely *must* become a customer? It's true that Bill Gates' name might be worth a truckload by itself, but I would assert that their values are pretty similar.

When thinking about the value of a given supporter to your company, influence and energy are equally important, as you can see in Figure 4.6. The person represented by point X, who is highly influential but minorly energetic, is just as valuable as the person represented by point Y, who is not very influential but is highly energized. Point A represents the ideal supporter, who is both powerful and energetic (think Oprah stumping for Obama during the 2008 election), and Point B represents a realistic combination that you should be seeking.

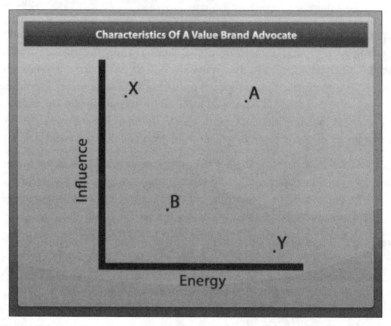

Figure 4.6 *Comparing influence and energy.*

Now that you know what to look for in a brand advocate, how do you find these people? Why would someone care about a company as much as they would care about, for example, their favorite celebrity, sports figure, or novel?

It has to begin with your own passion. If you are truly enthusiastic about your company, other people probably will be, too. Passion is magnetic. Probably the best piece of advice I got before my wedding is this: "Just have a great time. Your guests will enjoy the wedding as much as they see the bride and groom enjoying it." I think this advice applies in business equally well.

When you love your company, you want to share that feeling far and wide. Doing so on all the online platforms people use nowadays is important. But I recommend beginning with the real world. After all, the best offline advocates become the best online advocates. Attend events, host events, even sponsor events if you can. While you're there, strike up conversations. You don't need to talk to a specific number of people—just whomever you find yourself naturally speaking with. When you happen to be speaking to someone who seems to be a tastemaker, give them a bit of extra attention. And do not leave the conversation without offering to do something for them for free.

There is nothing quite like the power of free. People will eat food when they're not hungry just because it's free. They will save miniature bottles of shampoo that they don't need just because they're free from hotels. Recently, I carried a heavy bag of soil enricher home from a meeting because the guy I was visiting offered it to me as a gift. I don't even have any plants. And when people get something that's free that actually has value to them, they are very grateful. This is one way to create an advocate.

No matter what business you are in, there is some way to offer an influential person a bit of it at no cost. What that person may not notice is that, when someone takes something, there is an inherent desire to give back. And so, if influential persons like your product or service, they are more likely to tell people about it. But don't wait for them to do that. Ask them. Something along the lines of "Hey, I'm trying to build awareness about my new company. If you enjoyed the samples I gave you, do you mind tweeting about it?" would probably work well. It's tough to say no to a request like that. And both parties come out feeling good about it. It is likely that your new advocates will keep your company top of mind the next time they run into someone who could use the thing you sell.

Attending networking events and simply telling people about your product can also create advocates, but not nearly as quickly as when people are actively engaging with your product. True interaction with your brand—as long as people enjoy that interaction—is what leads to a loyal group of supporters. And it is that group that will carry your company in the coming age where online thoughts and opinions become direct leads for your business.

Winning the Real-Time Search Game

The point of the previous section is to make your company a part of people's social dialogue. As we start looking to search engines and social networks for recommendations on everything from nail salons to African safaris, you want your company to be on the tip of people's tongues—especially tastemakers, whose opinions are seen by many. If you build an active community of supporters, your company will be positioned to thrive when status updates are regularly returned as search results or social recommendations.

Google began experimenting with adding real-time results into the regular search results during its partnership with Twitter. Google+ status updates are next. Before long, real-time search will be a seamless part of social search rather than a separate entity.

Facebook has been noticeably absent from the real-time search world, but it is only a matter of time until it enters. Facebook probably won't build a real-time search engine like Google and Bing, but will use status updates to inform its social discovery product. Status updates allow Facebook to learn about you and therefore to deliver more relevant content, both in your user experience and in the ads you see. It is more likely Facebook will build some sort of social discovery tool into its home page or News Feed that serves you new content based on your friends' likes and interests.

It is unclear who the "winner" of the battle for real-time search market share will be, but it seems to me that it will be the company that is able to aggregate the most status updates and add the most customizations to real-time search. The larger the data set, the clearer the picture of the public's opinion on any given thing. And the more customizations, the more useful real-time search can be to the average person. Google is the natural frontrunner in this battle because of its ability to deliver the most relevant search results. This ability is fed by an equally great advantage: its massive processing power. The dozens of data centers that Google uses to process more than 24 petabytes of data per day will come in handy as the number of status updates swells.

Twitter could be a contender as well, given the fact that real-time search is in its DNA and people will always associate Twitter with public status updates. Plus, Twitter's partnership with Bing, which inserts tweets into Bing's search results, may give it extra power. But if Twitter is going to get serious about real-time search, it needs to open up its tweet backlog so more comprehensive searches can be performed and add more customizations. In my opinion, the only reason they are not already doing so is because of the processing power commitment it would require. Once again, we see the advantages of Google's riches.

Whoever the winner of real-time search ultimately is, the goal is the same for you, the marketer: get people talking about your brand in their status updates.

5

Where Social Meets Local

People need to find places near them in order to live their daily lives. We go out to eat, grab a cup of coffee, pick up groceries, see movies, go clothing shopping, get things printed, and various other everyday activities. We usually don't think much about how we decide which local place will serve our needs, but an entire industry is built around it.

The local industry used to be dominated by two sources: word of mouth and the Yellow Pages. You probably remember the days when you would use the Yellow Pages to find anything that you didn't already know about. Those days are over, thanks to Google. Personally, I think that's a good thing, because Google finds local places far quicker than a telephone book and gives us much more information, including other peoples' reviews of the place.

Local industry geeks classify local search into two categories: recovery and discovery. Recovery is finding information on a place you already know about. Discovery is figuring out a new place to go to. Google has pretty much dominated the recovery market. If you need to look up the address of the restaurant where you're meeting a friend, you'll probably go right to Google and type it in. Discovery, on the other hand, is still an open contest. Google owns a big slice of this market as well, because many people who are searching for a good shoe store in Philadelphia, as shown in Figure 5.1, will go to Google and type "shoe store philadelphia." But this experience leaves a lot to be desired.

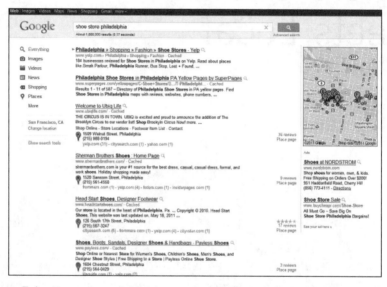

Figure 5.1 *A search result for "shoe store philadelphia" on Google. Although these results generally address the searcher's motivation, they have very little curation—that is, advice about which store would be best for you. Curation is best left to people in your social circle.*

The advent of social networks, and the recent groundswell of social data they have created, is a godsend to the local industry. Local stores are exactly the kind of thing that you would seek a recommendation on. I can't think of a single local category that I *wouldn't* consider a friend's advice about. Have I heard about that grocery store at the other end of town that has a world-renowned deli counter? No, but it sounds great. Do I know about the wine bar hidden on the thirtieth floor of a skyscraper that dispenses high-end wines from a row of glass machines? Crazy; I have to check that out.

The idea of other people scouring my neighborhood for me and recommending only the best places, which I can then try myself and make my own decisions about, is a shopping utopia. Fortunately, it is one that both Google and Facebook have their sights set on. In fact, much of this book was written in airports with free Wi-Fi sponsored by Google Places. In exchange for the Wi-Fi, I just had to view a screen asking me to rate and review the places I visited in the city where the airport is located.

The future of local search, where enough opinions have been contributed by users to create a custom-tailored local search for all, is sure to be exciting. Here is how I picture it looking:

In the ultimate local search, the first page of results would contain a fully personalized slate of recommendations from trusted friends. Not only would it tell me how many of my friends recommend each place and show me what they said about it, but it would report on what *people like me* thought of each place as well. As you will see throughout this book, I strongly believe that one of the best applications of social data is introducing us to the likes and interests of people who are similar to us (not to mention, to the people themselves—but that's an even bolder concept). After all, in such a big world, it is impossible to meet everyone. But if you could, you'd find a handful of people whose tastes are shockingly similar to your own, especially within certain areas like restaurants or movies. Comparing all your doppelgangers' different experiences to create a "best of" list would be incredibly valuable, even more so than a "best of" list from all your friends. Social data is slowly making this vision into a reality. More on that subject in Chapter 7, "The Possibilities of Social Data."

To get to a point where we have recommendations about almost every place in town from various people in our social circle, a lot more social data will be needed. This will come in time. I believe that people will want to volunteer more and more information about their tastes and preferences in order to create a "collective wisdom" for the people they care about.

But that's in the future. What we have right now—and what surely affects your income if you own a local business—is local search the way Google currently serves it.

How to Rank Highly in Google's Local Searches

The inner workings of the Google Places algorithm is a subject of much interest and debate in the local business community. The interest is understandable because the stakes are quite high; by some estimates, 20% of all Google searches are local.

For anyone who isn't familiar, local search results are the listings that show up above the regular Google search results with little red balloons next to them, often labeled A through G. Although I call them "local search" results, their technical name is Google Places results.

Despite the constant evolution of the Google Places algorithm, I can say with certainty, having performed more than a hundred tests on behalf of my clients, that a small group of factors determine which results show up at the top of the local results. These factors not only affect your listing's placement in Google Places search results, but also its likelihood of showing up if someone taps your local business's category, such as Restaurants, on Google's mobile home page (see Figure 5.2).

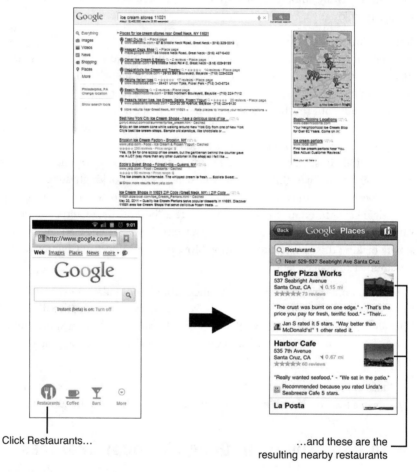

Click Restaurants...   ...and these are the resulting nearby restaurants

Figure 5.2 *A small group of factors determine what shows up at the top of the Google Places search results.*

The two most common scenarios in which people encounter Google Places results: search and mobile discovery. The top image is a resultset for a local category search (for example, "movie theaters atlanta" or "ice cream stores 11021") on a desktop computer. The images below are Google's mobile home page—which allows you to select a popular category so that Google can "discover" nearby places for you—and the personalized resultset that came from clicking Restaurants.

Following are all the major factors that determine a business's ranking in Google Places. They are roughly in order of importance.

✉ *Note: Social Factors Are Most Important*

I hope you'll find the following account of the current state of the Google Places algorithm helpful. However, keep in mind that it is a constantly shifting formula. If Google Places is important to your business, I recommend reserving your precious research time for one specific portion of the algorithm—social factors. The social portion of Google Places is the area that will see the greatest expansion in the coming months and years. Factors such as directory listings will soon take a back seat to social sharing, liking, and reviewing. On today's social web, Google is betting you want to see a place your friends like at least as much as one that their algorithm recommends. So all you Google Places optimizers, focus on the advice given in the previous chapters for building a network of supporters who will do status updates, shares, and mentions of your local business.

Directory Listings

Google did not create its database of local businesses by itself. It still relies, in part, on information and reviews from sources like Citysearch and Yelp. Therefore, it gives a great deal of respect to businesses that have presences on these and other local business directories. If you are serious about ranking your site at the top of the Places listings, the first thing you should do is publish listings on every business review site and directory you can find (see Figure 5.3). Keep in mind that only high-quality directories—often, ones that require you to pay—are trusted by Google. Also, make sure that you include the exact same business address, phone number, and website on every profile your business has across the Internet. This will indicate to Google that your business is a consistent and stable operation. Directory listings are to Google Places results as links are to organic search results. Translation: they're super important.

Figure 5.3 *A simple Citysearch.com profile like this one can boost your Google Places ranking as long as it contains the same address, phone number, and website listed elsewhere on the Web.*

Links

If your local business's website has links pointing to it from other websites, especially websites with a high TrustRank, it has a better chance of showing up at the top of the Google Places results. (For those who haven't read *Outsmarting Google*, TrustRank is the credibility Google gives to websites that allows them to rank higher. Your site earns TrustRank when other sites link to it and when your site is sufficiently aged.)

Proximity to the Searcher

Let's not forget that, no matter how great your website is and how many directory listings and links it has, it needs to be near the person performing the Google search. A fantastic restaurant in Poughkeepsie will not help a hungry searcher in Brooklyn. Although this factor is largely outside your control, the one way you can address it is by establishing your business in a dense area. The theory of being the only fisherman in a small lake generally doesn't work in business. You want to be fishing in a huge, well-stocked lake, even though there will be hundreds of fishermen competing with you. Do your best to outmaneuver them and you will be well fed. (Could anyone go for some filet of sole right about now? Just a thought.)

The importance of your business being close to as many people as possible has given rise to a kind of local search cheating. Lead-generation companies—businesses that make money by referring clients to other businesses—submit addresses to Google Places that they don't actually own. To bypass the verification process Google uses, they opt to verify by phone number, buying a cheap local number solely for the purpose of appeasing Google. (Local phone numbers also factor slightly into the Google Places algorithm.) They then create listings on every directory they can find and eventually make their way to the top of the Google Places rankings despite not actually being local businesses. Nowadays, anyone can use an offshore answering service to get a live person responding to phone calls 24/7. As a result, if someone calls one of these faux-local businesses, they may actually speak to someone they believe works at the business, making the scam even more convincing.

The same concept can be applied in a less-spammy but still improper way. Let's use Jasmine's Jewelry Store as an example. Jasmine might live in, say, Connecticut, but wants to create business for herself in a dense metropolis such as New York. So, in addition to the Google Places listing she has in Connecticut, she might pay the owner of a small business in midtown Manhattan a few bucks to receive mail to their address. Now that she has a Manhattan address, she creates a Google Places listing for her store in Manhattan, calling it Jasmine's Jewelry Store New York. When people click the listing, they see a great description with lots of pictures, but mysteriously, no pictures of the physical location in New York. Instead, they are directed to Jasmine's website, which is an e-commerce business. Jasmine's hope is that someone who was looking for a jewelry store in New York might come across her site and decide to purchase jewelry online instead. If she manages to rank well for a search like "jewelry store new york," her website traffic could increase significantly.

It's important to reemphasize that Jasmine's whole ploy would not work at all without some savvy in boosting her Google Places rankings. If she submitted her site to hundreds of directories, for instance, she might be able to get ahead in a short period of time. Many people take advantage of the many directory-submission services that exist in the underbelly of the SEO world. If you didn't own a local business, you'd be hard pressed to understand the purpose of a service where people or computer scripts submit your local business's information to hundreds of directories. After all, the links in these directories are all but worthless for organic SEO purposes, having been classified as low-quality links many years ago. But they still retain value for local SEO. If you google "directory submissions" you will see the many companies that participate in this trade. For those of you reading who are thinking about ordering from these companies, do so at your own risk. Google has known about them for years and is constantly getting better at detecting an unnatural pattern of directory appearances.

Business Name

A little-known (but heavily abused by those who *do* know) factor in Google Places rankings is the business name. If you own a Mexican restaurant in Chicago, for instance, and your name is Calientes, Google will not give your listing any more or less credibility based on business name alone. However, if you enter your business name in Google Places as The Great Chicago Mexican Restaurant, you instantly have a much better shot of showing up at the top of the Google Places rankings when someone searches "chicago mexican restaurants." Just as Google has classically ranked the dot com version of a keyword (such as chicagomexicanrestaurants. com) at the top of the organic results, it often places keyword-named businesses at the top of the Google Places rankings. This phenomenon occurs across all industries, from food and entertainment to medicine and law (see Figure 5.4).

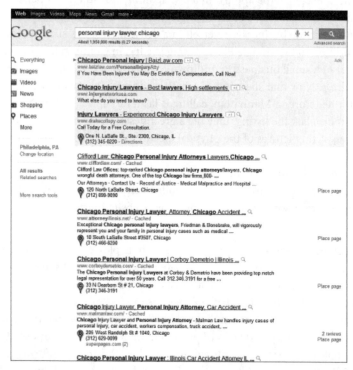

Figure 5.4   *Google Places gives a lot of value to businesses whose names match the keyword being searched. In a search for "chicago personal injury lawyer," every one of the first four listings in Google Places had the keyword in its business name.*

Proper Categorization and Tagging

Google values real human effort in their Places listings. For instance, if you have not manually verified your business through Google Places, you can forget your chances of showing up on the first page for any popular keyword. Similarly, if you have not categorized your local business properly, it will not show up for the keywords relating to your industry. You should fill out your business's Google Places profile fully.

Reviews

A small portion of the Google Places ranking algorithm depends on reviews. It's best to have at least 5–10, and even better if they come from different sources. Google includes reviews in a business's Places profile if they come from one of a few trusted sources such as TripAdvisor, Yelp, and Citysearch—or, of course, if the review is submitted on Google itself. Getting reviews is pretty easy. Simply ask your satisfied customers if they'd be kind enough to submit one.

> "...if you have not manually verified your business through Google Places, you can forget your chances of showing up on the first page for any popular keyword."

Social Interaction

Here is where local truly meets social. When friends rate, review, or +1 a local business, it will show up higher in the Places results. No matter where in the results a socially altered listing appears, the fact that there is extra information below the name of the listing (the preview of your friends' reviews of the place) calls the eye to it. To get more social interaction with your Google Places listing, I recommend asking your customers and website visitors to actively rate, review, and advocate for your business in any way comfortable for them. Posting a +1 button on your website is a low-hanging fruit, as is a link to your Google Places page with a call to action saying something like "Like what we're doing? Tell us on Google Places."

A correlated good idea is to keep a small group of customers for which you go above and beyond—either by providing them with more than they pay for, or by doing free work for them. I'm not saying to give away expensive services that require a big investment. In fact, anything at all that you do for no charge will create happy customers. These people then become the prime candidates to rate, review, +1, and generally root for your business on social networks (providing you ask them to do so).

An important caveat to the simple principle of asking people to support your company is that there must always be a feeling in each person that they are providing the support voluntarily. Put another way, you should ask people to evaluate your site, but not tell them *how* they should evaluate it.

Check-Ins and Location Sharing

Another factor that is sure to influence local search results is the ever-growing concept of check-ins. Check-ins are essentially pushing a button on your phone to broadcast your location—either generally, as in "Austin, Texas," or specifically, as in "Nettie's Crab Shack—2032 Union St., San Francisco." Typically, your check-ins would be announced through one of the popular check-in services: Foursquare, Gowalla, Twitter Places, and Facebook Places.

As silly as status updates originally seemed—"Let's tell everyone what I'm doing right now"—check-ins are perhaps even *more* unnecessary: "Let's tell everyone where I am right now." To some, they are yet another example of our society's movement toward a culture of constant attention seeking.

And with this increased desire for attention comes a further decline in privacy. Figure 5.5 shows a site that made a funny but serious point about the dangers of being so open about your location.

Figure 5.5   *A site called Pleaserobme.com, which, although no longer functional, allowed anyone to see a list of people who had "checked in" somewhere other than their home. Indeed, a few months later, a burglary ring used Facebook status updates to determine when people weren't home so it could rob them.*

Despite privacy implications, people are still checking in, and thus, there is a marketing opportunity. To begin with, check-ins may become a criteria for local searches. Google Places may, for instance, partner with Foursquare or Twitter to get check-in data and link it to your Gmail account to further personalize searches.

Even more likely is that Google will attempt to accumulate check-in data of its own by capitalizing on its powerful Android mobile platform. As our tolerance for openness continues to increase, people will become more comfortable with services like Google Latitude, which puts your location on a map for your friends and connections to see.

As I see it, a check-in would be factored into the Google Places algorithm slightly less than a review. In other words, if a friend of yours checked in somewhere, it might give that location a boost in the Google Places listings you see. However, that boost would not be as significant as a positive review or a +1 (or any kind of recommendation function Google invents in the future). A check-in means, "I've been there"; a positive review or +1 means, "I've gone there and so should you."

Check-ins on Facebook have an obvious use for local business owners. When you check in somewhere, your action of checking in—along with a link to the local business's page on the originating check-in service—has a chance of appearing on all your friends' walls. For that reason, a new form of viral marketing that many local businesses have begun pursuing is asking people to check in on their favorite service whenever they visit the establishment. As you can see in Figure 5.6, some have even gone so far as to post signs to the effect of, "Have you checked in yet? Get a special discount when you do." A virtual version of this same sign would appear on the local business's website.

Figure 5.6   *The kind of graphic that would appear in both a physical store and on its website, encouraging users to check in at the location. Doing so alerts the friends of all people who checked in that they visited the local businesses, which can bring in more customers.*

Encouraging customers to check in is a good idea for local businesses for a few reasons. First, it is an authentic act of loyalty. Without even saying how much you like a place, the simple act of broadcasting that you went there implies that you are proud of it. It reminds me of high school, when certain kids would announce at lunch that they had hung out at Joey The Popular Kid's house or went to a party at Carrie the Queen Bee's place. You didn't hear as much about their weekend when they spent it playing Jenga in the basement with their nerdy younger cousin.

Check-ins are particularly valuable for businesses that rely on tech-savvy males, because the majority of users who regularly check in fit that demographic. Marketing studies have also shown that these guys are particularly influential in their online communities. So, if your business receives a check-in, you can feel confident that it has far more value than the average marketing action (such as a Like on Facebook or a Follow on Twitter), providing you care about that particular demographic.

> "The reward is virtual rather than physical, but anyone who denies the effectiveness of virtual rewards is ignorant of the multibillion dollar online games industry."

Check-in services also act as a kind of built-in customer reward program for your local business: most check-in services, notably Foursquare, award badges and "mayorships" for visiting the same locations frequently. The reward is virtual rather than physical, but anyone who denies the effectiveness of virtual rewards is ignorant of the multibillion dollar online games industry.

Customers who check in are not only telling their friends about your business on various social networks, they will also be boosting your search engine rankings in the very near future. Bing has already publicly announced an intention to integrate check-ins into their social search, and Google is sure to do the same either through Google Latitude or whatever their ultimate check-in product turns out to be.

As a marketer, your obvious move—if you care about tech-savvy, influential males, at least—is to try to generate a lot of check-ins. How to do that?

- **Ask for them**—The most obvious strategy for attracting check-ins is the one I discussed earlier: ask your current customers to check in. You can do so in-store, online, or on your social media channels. That's the lowest hanging fruit.

- **Create specials**—On Foursquare and Facebook Places, you can offer specials—discounts or rewards—for customers who meet a certain goal that is beneficial to your business. Foursquare offers five kinds of specials: Friends, Swarm, Flash, Newbie, and Check-in. The Friend special incentivizes people to come with friends (see Figure 5.7). The Swarm special encourages people to come in groups during a limited time period, whether or not they know each other. The Flash special simulates a flash sale, where the special runs out after a certain number of people have claimed it. And the Check-in special is given to every customer who checks in.

Figure 5.7 *An example of a "Friends" special on Foursquare. Specials are a good way to encourage people nearby to visit your business.*

- **Add "tips" to locations**—Another interesting feature on Foursquare— one that exemplifies why the mobile social network is frequently referred to as a game—is that you can leave a "tip" at any location, meaning that when people are nearby, they will see a message that you have prepared. Typically, tips are used to tell users "secrets" about a local business, such as "Ask for the Whammy-Burger. It's not on the menu but they make it upon request." Tips are a great opportunity to build local folklore around your business, which, depending on exactly what your business is, could be a lucrative idea. When I ran my children's website, I would purposely hide "easter eggs," little surprises that you probably would never find unless you had been tipped off, all over the site. Because the site had a virtual currency called cartoon dollars, I would link these easter eggs to free cartoon dollars. An easter egg could be something as simple as a tiny logo thrown at the very bottom of the site, under the copyright information. When clicked, the logo would bring you to a screen that would flourish with light and announce: "You have stumbled upon a hidden place! 10 cartoon dollars have been added to your account." I would spread the word about the easter eggs by telling a few of the most gossipy kids on the site. I didn't have to do anything else. Soon there were whispers on the forum and even posts on other websites and blogs. The "secret" had gone viral.

I think adding similar kinds of easter eggs to your local business's website (again, that depends on what it is; if it's a law firm, ignore this advice), or even your physical store, has some really fun potential and is sure to get your company talked about.

Because of the cachet check-ins have earned in certain circles, many scheming users have attempted to increase their numbers artificially by checking in when they're not physically at the local business. It worked fantastically well back when check-ins were a Wild West. Recently though, Foursquare, Yelp, and most of the other check-in services have put restrictions in place to counteract this form of cheating. Typically, your phone will have to detect, via its internal GPS system, that you are actually at the location you're checking in to. Also, your past check-ins may be scrutinized for realistic behavior. For instance, you probably wouldn't check in to 20 places in one day. And finally, the local business's hours are often matched up with check-ins; a check-in when the business is known to be closed could result in a suspension of your account.

Contextual Discovery and the Local Landscape

One of the greatest manifestations of all this local data, from rating to reviews to check-ins, is the ability to make accurate, on-the-spot recommendations to users' mobile phones about where they should go, anywhere in the world. Google has this goal squarely in its crosshairs, both because it would be supremely useful and because it would be extremely profitable. If users begin to trust recommendations from Google on where to go and what to do, Goggle will have all but conquered the local market. And the advertising space next to those recommendations will become highly valuable, just like sponsored search results were back when most people couldn't tell the difference between them and the natural results.

Contextual discovery harkens back to the famed I'm Feeling Lucky button Google used to take so much pride in. For the small percentage of you who have never used the I'm Feeling Lucky button on Google (and, to be fair, it was marginalized when Google Instant was introduced in late 2010), it automatically brings the searcher to the first result for their search, bypassing the results page. It is basically a leap of faith that Google will find the perfect answer to the query.

 Note

Trivia Fact: Google was said to be losing $100 million each year because of the I'm Feeling Lucky button, as the skipped results page is where the advertising lies. That is the likely reason Google got rid of it when Google Instant came out.

The same principle of trusting Google's recommendations is at play with contextual discovery—which, to be clear, does not fully exist at the time of this printing. Google is inching toward it with its mobile home page, which allows you to click one of four icons—Restaurants, Coffee, Bars, and More—to get quick suggestions from Google Places. The evolution of contextual discovery will probably see users getting notifications on their phones offering them deals and highly personalized recommendations about local goings-on that they are likely to enjoy. In other words, it will fulfill Google's original description of contextual discovery: "search without searching."

One hopes that contextual discovery will fulfill every curiosity one has when visiting a new location—which, of course, varies depending on the individual. I, for instance, would want my phone to suggest the best hotels in whatever area I'm in as soon as I travel more than 100 miles from home. That's because I like hotels. My wife would want to be notified of any nearby theme parks. And my older brother would want to know the location of the nearest lobster joint. When I'm visiting a point of interest, I wouldn't mind having a virtual guide to tell me what I'm looking at. And when my phone detects that it's hotter than 80 degrees outside, I'd appreciate directions to the nearest ice cream shop. There is much more that a Google-equipped mobile phone could tell us about our location.

The optimization opportunity in contextual search will be clearer when we know where Google plans to get its local data. To date, they've been seeding their Places information with data from popular websites like Yelp, Citysearch, and TripAdvisor. It's not too much of a stretch to think that Google might partner with the established experts in various local fields, such as Frommer's for travel and Zagats for restaurants. And it could always pull data from the big daddy of Internet knowledge, Wikipedia. So, how do you make sure *your* local business is delivered as a notification to people's mobile phones when contextual discovery becomes a common thing?

Almost all of these sites rely on user-generated content. Yelp reviews are written by real people, as are TripAdvisor reviews. Frommer's and Zagats take the expert approach, but both accept user reviews on their websites, and I expect that user reviews will become even more prevalent in the future. (After all, people trust reviews over expert opinions in most categories nowadays.) So your opportunity to get more traffic during the era of contextual discovery relies on many of the same factors as your business showing up on Google Places today. Most notably, getting a lot of good reviews, having many incoming links to your website, and being referenced on numerous directories will secure your business's spot as an oft-"discovered" local place.

Social Data and the Local Meeting

When I was in college, I took a Psych 101 course with a very entertaining professor. I still remember some of the little gems I learned from that course. One of them, which I've quoted many times over the years, is that 30% of people end up marrying someone who grew up 10 blocks or less from them. Whether or not this percentage is accurate, it strikes me as more true than most of us realize.

I've thought often about what this statistic means. Does it mean that our most important commonalities come from where we grew up? Or does it mean that there is someone compatible for us in every group of a few hundred people? Whichever of these speculations is true, the local area is definitely a place of great potential. This is why I consider bringing people together in local areas to be one of the great unlocked potentials of the Internet.

To date, I know of two websites that accomplish this goal successfully: Meetup.com and Craigslist. But neither site uses the incredible potential of social data to match up people with common interests. They rely on people actively reaching out and seeking social activities. The reality is, for every ad placed on Craigslist for a tennis partner or hiking group created on Meetup.com, 99.9% of the people who would be a good match for these meetings never hear of it. What we need is less search and more discovery.

If Facebook—or any third-party application using Facebook's database—compared the likes and interests of every person within a 20-mile radius and invited people to partake in real-life activities, a new era of socialization would be born. And in a way, a significant loop would be closed: the one where the Internet not only connects us with more people, but fosters real social activity between them rather than virtual social activity. I believe we will see some insightful entrepreneur create the

Pandora.com of people one day: a "friend discovery" site that doesn't feel forced, which relies on the incredible amount of data we have been feeding Facebook and other social networks for years. Yes, the solution will have to be elegant; most people can't be bothered to leave the house and meet new people. But the right set of hands will eventually come along and wake this sleeping giant.

Most likely, Facebook will not be the one to do it, for two reasons. First, fostering in-person interaction takes people away from using Facebook. Second, Facebook has always aligned itself with a vision of reuniting actual friends rather than helping you to make new friends. And so, it would have to be a third-party application using Facebook's data or another website with a large userbase. (If the CEO of Meetup.com is reading this, email me.)

Because I am speaking so much about Meetup.com, I must mention what I think is one of the best and most underused marketing tactics: creating a real-life group related to your business. You wield far more marketing power when speaking to a group of people in person than you do posting to people's status streams on a social networking site. Suppose you have a company that sells running shoes. Go to Meetup.com, Craigslist, or any other active community-building site and establish a group for people who love running. If you don't have time to run this group, ask someone else at your company to do it. But you will definitely find that, if you can get 30 people to actively participate in your group, you will have 30 marketing opportunities that come about completely organically. At some point in your conversation with each of the people in your group, it will probably come up that you own a running shoe company, and people will feel compelled to learn more. You will never have that person's attention in any online context as much as you do during that in-person conversation.

There is a way to involve almost any kind of company in a real-life group. It just takes some creativity. If you own a web design firm, you could start a meetup for entrepreneurs or first-time business owners. They all need websites. The same group would work if you owned an insurance company. Many business owners would need insurance. If you have a pizza store, you could start a pizza lovers group that meets at your shop once per week to socialize and make new friends. If you have a jewelry business, you could start a daytime social club for women who like to lunch. Women who don't work who have the time to go to frequent lunches may be good potential customers. In short, think about the demographic of your customers and choose an interest that links most of them, especially if that interest directly relates to your company.

You may notice that this book increasingly contains advice about activating people in real life rather than taking a purely online approach. That is because I see the online world bringing people physically together more and more in the future, especially with mobile phones becoming the center of social activity whenever people are outside the house. With the Internet leading to greater real-life socialization, I also see optimization in the traditional "tricking the algorithms" way becoming a thing of the past. There will always be a Wild West to conquer or a system to beat, but focusing on a personal marketing strategy that will never expire can be a better investment of time.

In the future, as in the past, individuals who form an affinity with a brand or organization will become the secret sauce to boosting sales. This was a core principle of marketing before the Internet came along, and it will continue to be. When speaking about Internet marketing, I often say that everything—and nothing—has changed. In the local category, genuine recommendations and expressions of loyalty will always be the strongest driver of sales. These actions have mostly migrated to the online world, but in truth, it is only the medium and not the method that has changed.

> "In the future, as in the past, individuals who form an affinity with a brand or organization will become the secret sauce to boosting sales."

So as online-savvy as you become, work on becoming people-savvy, too (and if you're not the type, partner with someone who is). In the local market, nothing could serve you better. As you will see in the next few chapters, brands of every size will continue to need a band of loyal supporters in order to thrive on the social Internet.

6

Converting Social Media into Profits

Because I do a lot of public speaking about marketing, I am always interested in watching fellow speakers to see what advice they give. Strangely, I find that most of them never broach the topic of making money through social media. I have even seen speeches about making money through social media that don't talk about how to make money through social media. Instead, I hear a lot of "join the conversation," "engage your audience," "be human," and other platitudes that don't achieve much more than sounding clever. Either the majority of these speakers don't know how to covert traffic into profits or they consider it a huge secret.

I don't claim to be a master of every way of earning money online, but I do know quite a few methods that have worked well for the eight years that I've been an entrepreneur. In this chapter, I will share some of them with you. I don't mind doing so for the simple reason that all of them involve a good amount of effort, and if you are willing to put in the work, you deserve to succeed. After all, there is no such thing as easy money in life, and the truly motivated among you will do well whether I share my secrets or not.

Making Yourself Valuable

Social media is the grease, not the wheel. Unless you sell social media services (guilty!), the only purpose of social media for businesses is to facilitate the sale of a product or service. Therefore, before you even get into the ways of influencing search engines or social networks, you must have a good product. And often, *you* are part of the product.

A good product should either be needed or wanted. If you sell swimsuits, they should fit right, look good, or both. If you sell web design, it should be functional, attractive, or both. You can't sell something that people don't need or want. However—and this is a big however—you have tremendous influence over whether people *think* they need or want something. I could give you many examples, but I will invoke just one: the pet rock (see Figure 6.1). The pet rock, a simple stone in a box that requires no maintenance whatsoever, made its owner a millionaire. In this concept, we see that the marketing can matter much more than the product. The creator of the pet rock was selling his marketing ingenuity far more than he was selling a product that anybody actually needed.

> "...you have tremendous influence over whether people *think* they need or want something."

Figure 6.1   *The pet rock proves that the way you market your product can outshine the inherent value of the product.*

Your value to your own business is huge. There are certain people who can sell anything. There are others who are master organizers. Still others are master executors. Some of my favorite business owners simply know how to hire people smarter than themselves.

If you sell swimsuits that don't look good or fit well, but you are a charismatic person who makes everyone feel great, you can still make money. If you sell web design that is dysfunctional and ugly, but you market it as "starter web design at a ridiculously low price," your company could succeed. On the other hand, if you have the greatest product in the world but don't know how to market and sell it, not only could you fail—you are *bound* to fail. Time after time, we see that the pitch is as important as the product.

> "Time after time, we see that the pitch is as important as the product."

The best combination of assets for a business to have, of course, is a great product *and* great marketing. And truly talented marketers know how to make themselves valuable.

So what do I mean by "making yourself valuable"? I mean possessing something of value: a skill, a quality, even a possession. If you have something that people want, not only will social media be kind to you, but every relationship you make will stick better and yield more benefits. The idea of making yourself valuable is where old marketing ("tell your friends") and new marketing ("post about it online") come together. As friends begin to influence the purchases you make via social search results, social discovery, and social ads, your personal relationships are becoming more important than ever before.

As discussed in Chapter 2, "The New Influences in Search and Social Media," it is not just the number of relationships you have, but the esteem in which your friends hold you that determines your influence in social media. That is, you don't only want to be a "friend"; you want to be a tastemaker.

The things that will make you into a tastemaker online are the same things that make you popular offline. They are basically the qualities that cause people to be attracted to one another. Although the following list may not be new to you, it would be remiss of me to exclude it when giving advice about how to gain clout in the era of social media.

- **Money**—It's amazing how much will people will look up to someone just because that person has money. The person didn't even have to have earned it. Look to reality TV if you need some examples.

- **Beauty**—It is a sad truth that something you were born with (or bought) can help you meet more people and sell more products. Case in point: When I was eleven years old, I was in my local flea market when I passed by a beautiful girl who was probably sixteen, working at a jewelry booth. Since I was scared to death of girls at that time, I walked by as quickly as possible. However, I caught her smiling at me out of the corner of my eye. "Hey," she said. I was arrested. "Hi," I muttered, pausing in my tracks. "Do you want to try on this leather bracelet?" she asked. "I need to sell a bunch of them. Plus it would look really cool on you." Being the most straight-edge mama's boy ever, I had absolutely no desire for a leather bracelet. But desire was a confusing concept right about then. She tied the bracelet around my wrist, allowing her hand to briefly touch mine. I left that day with two leather bracelets.

- **Intelligence**—Although not as important as the preceding two when it comes to business relationships, it can earn respect. It is in the category of money and beauty, however, because it is a quality that you are born with that other people desire.

- **Charm**—The best salesperson I know is a longtime friend named Reed. He is a handsome guy, but does not take advantage of the other two qualities: there is nothing flashy or "rich-looking" about him, nor does he tout his intelligence in any noticeable way. The crazy thing is, when you're around him, you just feel good about yourself. He makes you feel like you just got accepted into the popular clique in high school, and you find yourself feeling so drawn into that feeling that you end up wanting to do business with him.

- **Connections**—The most humdrum, nonchalant person you know could go from zero to hero if he suddenly became Oprah's personal assistant. Why? Because he is close to someone with the ultimate perceived value. It is the same with people who know lots of other people. No matter how valuable people think you are in a business context, you become even more valuable if you are associated with desirable people.

- **Ability**—If you are particularly good at any one thing, people will want to know you. This is why, back when I owned a college consulting business, I would always tell kids to be "pointy" rather than well-rounded when applying to schools. It is more desirable to excel at any one thing than to be pretty good at many things. For instance, if you could sink a basketball shot from the other end of the court 9 out of 10 times, most people would want to know you, even if you weren't good at anything else. It would just be cool to know someone who was "blessed" in a certain way, however impractical his ability might be. Applied to a business context, it is best if this ability has something to do with business (number crunching whiz, idea man, superb writer), but in truth *any* ability will impress some people.

- **A Mysterious Self-Confidence**—Absent any other form of business value, if you simply believe in yourself a lot, people are going to be taken aback and want to be around you. Back when I ran my kids' website, I allowed myself to be pitched by a guy who wanted to put spammy advertisements on my site. I had zero interest in him doing so, but something about his email made me respond. I told him, politely, thanks but no thanks. Yet he insisted that a few minutes on the phone was all he wanted, and I bit. Rather than being begged for an opportunity, I found myself speaking to someone who took immediate control of the conversation in a nonthreatening way. He began the conversation by asking me whether I was happy with my life. Although I felt taken off guard, I eventually found myself thinking, "What an interesting guy." Ultimately, I still refused to allow his ads on my site, but I ended up building a relationship with him that lasts to this day. As valuable people go, he is an interesting outlier, because he offered me nothing beyond pure intrigue.

I am hoping that you identified some of these attributes as characteristics of yourself. But even if you don't have most of them, there is no need to worry. First, you can always "fake it to make it." Sometimes acting like you have these characteristics can earn them for you in time. (But be careful not to be insincere, because it's easily detectable by most.) But more importantly, you can outshine any of these qualities by working hard and caring about what you do.

Also worth noting is that, despite my statement that the pitch can be more valuable than the product, the product can do a lot of work on its own if it's useful or interesting enough. A puppy salesman, for instance, does not need to be very charismatic.

The Principles of Selling Through Social Media

After you have a product and a network of people to share that product with, how do you make money? The simplest answer: Learn how to sell.

Many people who are personable, charming, and even persuasive are not good salespeople. It is a subtle art to request that another person part with hard-earned money for something that you possess. It requires a certain level of confidence; for in effect, you aren't just saying, "My product is worth it"; you are saying, "I am worth it."

I have met many a salesperson at a cocktail party who has told me that the product or service he sells is quite useful and interesting, but I simply didn't believe him. The conversation usually goes something like this:

Me: "So, what do you do?"

Guy: "I sell ads for a tech news website."

Me: "Oh, neat. Do you enjoy that?"

Guy: "I do. It's interesting work, and we've got a really great team. Our company just acquired another website so we're shuffling around quite a bit, creating some new packages for our advertisers."

Me: "So, you're not just selling banner ads and stuff?"

Guy: "Oh, far from it. We do all kinds of integrative work, product placement and such. It's really in-depth. You own a social media company, right? You should check it out. I'll give you a discount if you're interested in trying us out."

Me: "Oh cool, that sounds good. Let me get your business card and we'll definitely connect."

...Huh? What? Oh I'm sorry, I think I may have just fallen asleep while I was writing. Although the guy in that conversation ostensibly did his job, he did not actually engage me or give me any reason to buy what he was selling.

A good salesperson will always figure out the goals of a potential customer so that he can tailor his pitch to them. If the guy from that conversation was a great salesperson, he would have asked me what type of clients I'm looking to attract, what I hope to achieve in the next year, and what I like most about my job. He would have gotten a feel for me on a business level *and* on a personal level, dexterously switching between personas until I felt like he was a friend who happened to have a really great product to sell. He would then entice me with the power of story—mentioning a key client or two who are in the same field as me and made a killing from those ads that he sells. Finally, he would completely switch the topic so I didn't feel like he was trying too hard. But a day or two later, I'd find a reminder of my new friend in my inbox, an email asking if I'd like to go to lunch sometime or maybe grab a drink. During one of the next few occasions we see each other—all of them pleasant, all of them building in me a feeling of trust—he'd close the deal.

When selling a product through social media, the same principles apply. The difference is a lack of personal interaction. Not being able to feel someone's energy in person is a major drawback, but it can be made up for by conforming to the type of interaction people like to have online. Everyone's in-person self is different from their online self, and understanding this distinction is crucial to selling in today's Internet-driven world.

Following are the five key principles to selling online in the social age, as I see them:

Principle #1: Cater to Short Attention Spans

The main difference between online and offline is the amount of choices available. In real life, you can be in only one place at a given time. You are limited by what the eye can see. Online, however, you can be many places at once: shopping in a boutique, at a concert watching your favorite band, in a "room" with your friends, and inside the world of an addictive game. Because of the endless choices you have, you become pretty picky about where you place your attention.

Long-form writing is seldom read online, except on tablet devices. In 1990, you might have been more tolerant of lengthy correspondences, such as the eight-paragraph letter that your aunt sent you in the mail. But in 2012, that same letter is probably going to be a quarter of the size, and if it isn't, it has very little chance of being read. With the explosion of interesting content online, our attention spans have shrunk. Therefore, if your message isn't sufficiently snappy and interesting, very few people will ever read it in its entirety.

Figure 6.2 contains two versions of the same message, both well written. One is 143 words long and the other, 23 words. Can you guess which is more effective?

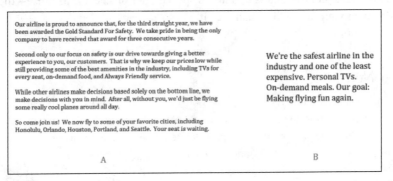

Figure 6.2 *Two ways of saying the same thing. Message A conveys more information but is less likely to be read because of its length. Message B is shorter—it could even fit within Twitter's parameters of "140 characters or less"—and it makes the same basic points.*

Principle #2: Know Your Medium

Communicating effectively on your social media channels is a deceptively difficult task. Many a well-intentioned marketer has posted a status update on his or her Facebook business page to the tune of: "20% of all widgets from now until Friday! Click here to take advantage of this special sale!" Predictably, that status update resulted in zero sales. That's because people don't like to be pitched out of the blue. If they come to you looking to purchase something, they don't mind a pitch. But if they're busy doing other things and you interrupt their day to recommend your product, you won't get much response at all. Posting about a sale on Facebook is equivalent to the latter situation because people are acting social on Facebook: browsing pictures, commenting on each other's walls, and catching up with friends. They are probably not interested in hearing about a sale during that time.

Instead, you want to make your brand fit in better. No matter what you sell, you should be asking your fans how their day is going, what the weather is like where they live, and how they feel about the latest news story. By simply relating to your fans in a way that is personal and sincere, you are becoming that guy or gal that everyone enjoys being around. Chances are, next time they are thinking about buying the thing you sell, your company will cross their mind. Not only will this down-to-earth behavior cause people to enjoy their interactions with your company more, but it will trigger positive actions such as liking, commenting, and sharing, which will cause your status updates to show up higher on people's News Feeds. There is even a name for the act of vying for likes and comments in order to appear higher in the News Feed: EdgeRank Optimization. EdgeRank is the algorithm Facebook uses to order the status updates in your stream.

The biggest benefit of your page blending in with people's lives better is that when you *do* sprinkle in a business update—a special offer or sale, for instance—the majority of your fans will actually see it.

 Note

Post business-related status updates only about one in every six updates, and do so during the work day when people are more open to thinking about business. (This rule applies less strongly to inherently social businesses such as restaurants and lounges.)

Here are some categories of status updates that tend to get responses from the Facebook community:

- Discussing a big sports game
- Asking about a phone, iPod, or other electronic device that many people own
- Telling a story that is universally understood (about loving or hating weather conditions, how difficult it is to find parking in the city, or the deliciousness of a popular food like pizza)
- Making a quip about a celebrity who is currently in the news

When you feel you have maximized your EdgeRank, getting at least 10–20 likes and comments on each of your status updates, you have done all you can to get your page to show up high in people's News Feeds. From that point, your focus should be on creating worthwhile business updates and measuring the number of people that click through to your business page and make a purchase. The alternative to posting occasional business-related status updates, which, though painstaking, is probably the most effective way of utilizing your newly expanded Facebook relationships, is to message people privately. An inbox message that gently mentions your interest in doing business with a "friend" is the most effective way to make sales using Facebook. (Just remember not to pitch your real friends on Facebook or you won't have any left.)

Generating sales through Twitter is similar in its approach, but Twitter has a slightly different culture. Because it is a public social network—in contrast to Facebook, which emphasizes sharing only with "friends"—people respond to a different kind of message. Twitter is viewed more as a repository of interesting links, concise thoughts, and tidbits from intriguing people. And so, when writing a status update for Twitter, you shouldn't be quite as personable and friendly as you would be on Facebook. Instead, your message should be more snackable. Quotes still work well, as do links to articles with clever titles, and strong opinions.

Here are some tweets that I believe would have a high rate of interaction:

When was the last time you saw one of these? 1981? http://bit.ly/12234.

Never...trusting...weather report...again. http://bit.ly/12323.

"Luck is preparation meeting opportunity."—Oprah Winfrey

Trusting a politician is like leaving a wolf in charge of your flock of sheep.

As you can see, the first two quotes are meant to entice the reader to click a link. The third is meant to be a timeless quote that people find to be wise, and therefore retweet (repeat to their followers). And the fourth is meant to be universally relatable, with the hope that people will retweet it or reply to it.

Unlike Facebook, Twitter does not have an algorithm that determines the order of status updates; they are all sorted chronologically, with the most recent at the top of the list. The purpose of writing charismatic status updates on Twitter is to attract followers and start conversations. These actions will facilitate relationships with new people and deepen relationships with current followers. Ultimately, you want to convert your Twitter relationships to email, phone, or in-person relationships so you can close sales.

Principle #3: Target People's Core Interests

Because of the minimal amount of time and attention each marketing message receives online, it is crucial to make good use of your opportunity. First of all, be sure you're talking to the right people. It simply isn't economical to pitch people who aren't interested in what you're selling. If you can manage to cut out the masses of uninterested parties and concentrate only on potential customers, the number of qualified leads to your business will skyrocket. Second, you should be identifying the other interests of your potential customers. There's nothing wrong with baiting people in with something they're *more* interested in than what you're selling. And third, you always want to approach people in a way that is comfortable for them, in terms of timing, tone, and ease of interaction. Even the ideal product can become undesirable if offered at the wrong time or through unpleasant means.

> "If you can manage to cut out the masses of uninterested parties and concentrate only on potential customers, the number of qualified leads to your business will skyrocket."

Whatever your messaging medium—Facebook, Twitter, YouTube, Google Ads, or email—targeting is key. However, it is difficult to target specific groups of people through most of today's social media channels. On a personal Facebook profile, you can separate people into groups so that only the people you've selected receive your status updates. However, this is a manual process and requires one-by-one selection of friends into custom groups. An alternative is to create different Facebook accounts for each group you want to target, but this is not only against Facebook's terms of service, it can't be done feasibly for more than two or three target groups, because your multiple identities will confuse people who wish to friend you. It works best if you have two discrete aspects of your life—suppose you are a musician and a marketer—and want to completely segregate the people you know in each area.

Facebook business pages do not even allow this level of targeting: the only filters you can apply to your status updates are location and language. If you really want to target, you have to create multiple business pages and attract different kinds of people to each page using advertising. On Facebook, you can choose to send your *personal* status updates to a specific group of people (see Figure 6.3). The drop-down menu underneath the status update field has an option to "Customize," which allows you to create and store a group of people to which your status updates are exclusively sent.

A business page, in contrast to a personal page, only allows you to target status updates to people in a particular location or who speak a certain language (see Figure 6.4). Unfortunately, Facebook probably withholds brands' ability to do better-targeted status updates so as not to compete with its advertising platform. You can find this option through the "Customize" button under the status update field on your business page.

Twitter does not have a targeting feature, but you can easily accomplish it using a third-party service; just google "twitter group app" and you'll find plenty. As with a Facebook personal page, you will have to individually curate which users go into each group.

On YouTube, there is also no way to share your video with a specific group of people, but the solution is easy enough: change the video to "unlisted" in your settings and then share the video with specific groups of people through email or Facebook.

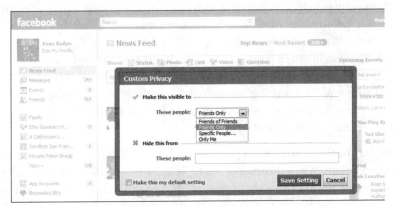

Figure 6.3   *Facebook allows you to send personal status updates to a specific group of people.*

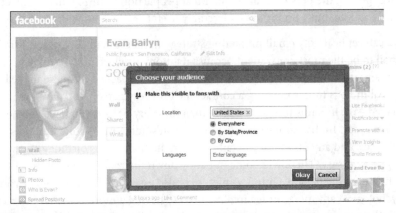

Figure 6.4   *Facebook's business pages are more limited, only allowing you to target status updates to people in a particular location or who speak a certain language.*

Targeting using the previous methods may seem a bit painstaking, but the work ethic involved is the difference between what the 5% of people who profit from social media do and what the other 95% do. However, you will be glad to know that two other marketing strategies are a much more natural fit for targeted social media campaigns—Facebook ads and email.

Facebook ads are far and away the most granular method of targeting in existence; you can advertise only to 37-year-old male teachers from Indianapolis who like fly-fishing if you want. Or, if that group doesn't tickle your fancy, you can target female architects between the ages of 40 and 60 who live in New York and like landscaping. Again, there is nothing like it.

While demographic targeting has been around for a while, psychographic targeting—that is, targeting by interest—is relatively new to the online landscape. Before Facebook came along, if you wanted to reach people who have a particular interest, you either had to advertise on a niche website or put together an email or mailing list by hand. These older methods might still be effective, but Facebook targeting has set a new standard in targeting. As a result, the potential of Facebook ads is greater than that of any advertising product since Google AdWords. I have dedicated Chapter 8, "Dominating Facebook Ads," entirely to advertising on Facebook, so I will leave that topic alone for the moment and focus instead on the other best way of targeting online: email.

Email may be the clearest, most personal, and most reliable way to get someone's attention online. When it comes to selling "cold" (in contrast to "warm" selling, where people already know about your product or service), it's about as efficient and effective as it gets. In fact, the main form of marketing that I employ revolves around email. I simply use my Gmail contacts list to the max, turning each contact into a Rolodex on steroids: a detailed account of my entire knowledge of, and relationship with, the person in question. Most people don't utilize Gmail contacts as heavily as I do, but I find it to be incredibly useful.

You can replicate my email marketing strategy in most email clients, but I find Gmail to be the most convenient because it automatically syncs your contacts to most smartphones, turning your phone into a power-packed resource for selling. All there is to it is creating a contact file for every person you have ever emailed—or, if that is too great a task, then for every person you have emailed in the past year. In that contact file, list the person's full name, phone numbers, email addresses, and any other juicy details you can dig up, such as birthday and wedding anniversary. These will come in handy down the road, when you want to stay at the top of the person's mind. A picture is also essential, because it gives you the psychological advantage of feeling like you are having a more personal interaction with the contact each time you email. Besides this "basic" information on your contact, you should also have a detailed field that includes a brief bio of the contact and a short history of your communications. Filling out each contact can take five or more minutes. But the investment pays off in spades when you add labels to each contact, thereby prepping them for a targeted email campaign.

In Gmail, labels are called Groups. I have groups for each industry, geographic area, and relationship category. Some of my industry groups are Green/Organic,

Marketing, PR, Design, Nonprofit, and Authors. Some of my geographic groups are New York, San Francisco, Los Angeles, Philadelphia, Texas, UK, and Australia. As you can see, I sometimes use cities and sometimes use states or even countries. Because I have fewer contacts in certain areas, this makes sense for me. I only have several dozen contacts in Texas, for instance; however, I have hundreds of contacts in California, spread throughout San Francisco, Los Angeles, and San Diego, so I need a group for each city.

The "relationship category" groups are the most creative, and often the most useful. Some of my relationship category groups are Evan Advocates, Big Shots, Fortune 500s, Best Of Class, and Leads. The Leads group is particularly practical for me, since, with the push of a single button, I can see every contact I am currently following up with about a contract. I take advantage of this group almost every day when I'm going through the list of people with whom I have an active sales relationship. The Evan Advocates group has also proven valuable, because, when I need a favor, such as a vote in an online contest, I know I can rely on this group to spread the word. Best Of Class is another interesting group. It is my coveted list of those rare people I meet who are brilliant at what they do, the folks that I would love to place at the head of a department in the imaginary supercompany I plan to create one day.

When I am giving a speech in a particular city, or developing a social media product that is an ideal fit for an industry, it is very easy for me to reach out to the right people. The groups are a lifeline to me. That is why I say that when it comes to targeting, email has an advantage that no other medium can touch. I have complete freedom with how I organize my contacts (unlike with Facebook, for instance) and it is easier to translate my interactions into sales because most people read their email every day and use it as a primary method of communication. Although a lot of work goes into maintaining my contact list, I've found it to be one of the most profitable projects I've undertaken.

Figure 6.5 shows one of my Gmail contact pages, which contains all the contact information I would ever need, as well as notes on the person and our history together. The most important part of the contact, however, is the "groups." I have placed this person, Derek Babb, into "Evan Advocates," "Games," "Marketing," and "San Francisco."

Figure 6.5 *Note that you can gather Gmail contacts into specific groups, allowing you to easily contact specific groups of people.*

Having covered the targeting techniques that I find most effective, I want to encourage you to develop your own. Here are two inventive ideas that should get your creative juices flowing.

- **Personal Google Ad targeting**—Looking to get in touch with someone in particular? Or a company in particular? Purchase their names as keywords and say something special to them (see Figure 6.6).

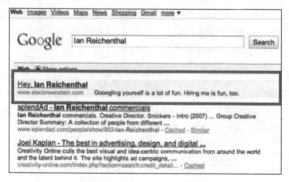

Figure 6.6 *Use a personal Google ad to target a specific person.*

- **Twitter image wordplay**—On any public Twitter page, images of the last five people that followed that account are displayed. You can have some fun with this fact by creating five Twitter accounts and making the profile image of each of them into a letter or two so that the grouping of the images forms a word or short sentence. When you click any of the letters in the images, you land on a profile page that can display your contact information, sales info, or whatever else you want. That is how the clever rascal shown in Figure 6.7 attracted the attention of an executive whom he wanted to give him a job.

 Note

A variation of this technique is separating an image into five segments and using each one as a different profile picture so that you can effectively place an image of your choosing onto anyone's profile.

Figure 6.7   *Clever usage of Twitter images can grab attention.*

Principle #4: Ask for the Sale

I have already emphasized the importance of asking for things, and this point will come up again in Chapter 8 in the context of Facebook ads. But it is worth mentioning again as a general principle of online sales.

Experience has taught me that people buy things only if they are actively convinced to do so. It's sort of like the law of physics that states that objects don't move unless they have a force acting on them. A rock perched at the edge of a cliff will not fall unless something pushes it. Similarly, a visitor to your website will not purchase anything unless something on the website moves him to do so.

You can convince people to make purchases through many means. Anxiety, desire, ambition, guilt, ego, and simplicity. (I call this set of psychological characteristics ADAGES. For a full explanation of ADAGES, see the following chart.) Asking visitors to make purchases on your website falls into the category of Simplicity; it is such a basic form of persuasion that many people overlook it.

So why is asking so powerful? Mainly because people like to take the clearest and least confusing path. The slightest bit of hassle can turn someone off from doing something.

Let me ask you something. Would you like a smoothie right now? If the answer is yes, then let me ask you another question: Would you like to get off your chair, put on your shoes, find your car keys and wallet, drive to the store, find parking, order a smoothie, stand in line, pay the cashier, wait for the smoothie to be prepared, get back in your car, drive home, park, take off your shoes again, and get back in your chair? The answer to that question is probably no. Heck, it sounds like a lot of work. But if that process could be simplified; if you could push a button and get a smoothie instantly, then the answer would revert back to yes pretty quickly. In fact, you'd probably find yourself drinking a lot more smoothies.

The effects of instant gratification can be felt especially powerfully online. You literally *can* push a button and get what you want (well, almost). And in an environment that is so tempting, those who make the purchasing process easier come out ahead. That is why advertising campaigns that involve an ask—otherwise known as a "call to action"—are so much more effective than campaigns without them. "20% off all designer jeans today" is a far cry from "20% off all designer jeans today. Click to claim yours now." The second version eliminates the moment of confusion where the viewer wonders, "How?"

Here are some examples of effective asks within website copy and ads:

- Our bagels are fresh, delicious, and baked daily. **Won't you bring some home today?**
- Here at Resume Builders, we believe that a good resume is the first step in a successful career. **Call us now to begin writing your future.**
- Enzo's Wine Bar. Sit back. Relax. **Have a glass on us.**
- Do you believe this government should step out of our affairs? So do we. **Donate $25 to Freedom Lovers Association now.**

THE SIX UNDERLYING REASONS WHY PEOPLE MAKE PURCHASES (ADAGES)

Anxiety—What stronger motivator of purchases is there than the hope of relieving some of the anxiety we all carry around inside of us? The news industry tells us, "If you don't purchase a newspaper or watch our programming, you might miss a story that would have kept you safer." The alcohol and pharmaceutical industries tell us, "If you feel bad about yourself, come take comfort with our product and you'll feel much better."

Desire—People make buying decisions based on physical attraction all the time. The effectiveness of sex in ads has been explored in many a psychological study and undergraduate term paper. Calvin Klein knows it. American Apparel knows it. And so do hundreds of other companies that pique people's desire in their ads.

Ambition—A lot of people like to buy "up": they purchase things that set them up for a better life. A fancy business-card holder, a sharp suit, a flashy car. Some of these purchases fall into the category of Ego, but others are made simply to surround themselves with things that paint the picture of a grander life.

Guilt—Purchases are made out of guilt all the time. Gifts are often a way of saying "I'm sorry" and "I wish I were there." Companies can also induce guilt by putting forth messages about what you ought to be doing. The green industry is a good example of an industry that is fueled largely by (rightful) guilt. Its basic message: "We're destroying our planet. Won't you do your part by buying green products?"

Ego—How clever many a liquor company is, portraying a version of their ideal customer in their ads, but altering that customer to make him seem cooler, more liked, and more fun. The ads mean to arouse a subconscious "That's me!"—but with a leap of faith that you are just a tad more awesome than you actually are. The fashion industry is another one that is all about ego, essentially saying, "Wear our clothes. You'll look good and people will be attracted to you."

Simplicity—As much as the average person enjoys acquiring stuff, the desire to unclutter, to streamline, to simplify, is a strong driver in many people's lives. The Web is an especially dense environment, with trillions of bits of content floating around across tens of millions of websites. In such a crowded setting, a clear and direct path is always a welcome reprieve. Even if a store is crowded, if you can easily find what you want and buy it without hassle, the Simplicity idea has been achieved. Case in point is Amazon.com. The interface may not be gorgeous, but how often do you have trouble finding what you want? Amazon has gotten searchability and availability nailed, showing you the popularity of the item on the page, what people ultimately bought after they visited the page, and similar items you might also be interested in. The shopper rarely feels confused and can easily make purchases. Other good examples of web stores that have nailed simplicity are iTunes and Zappos.

Principle #5: Invest Widely in Small Quantities, Then Invest Deeply in Whatever Is Working

This is one of the most basic principles in marketing: see what works, and when you find out what does, keep putting money into it. Whenever I speak to a company that has never experienced top organic rankings on Google, I give them this advice: "Try it. Invest enough to get a few keywords to the top of Google. After you see the benefits, you can expand the campaign if you're making more than you're spending, and if you're not, then drop it."

The same advice could be applied to any form of marketing or advertising, providing it makes *some* intuitive sense for the business. You won't interest a dog food manufacturer in advertising in a rare coins magazine, but you might interest them in a mailer campaign that delivers letters to everyone in a family friendly neighborhood. Maybe he wouldn't have thought of spending his marketing dollars in that way, but he should probably try it on some scale.

In the age of social media, your options are greater than ever before. Most businesses should try Google ads, Facebook ads, PR, email marketing, niche website advertising, sponsoring or producing industry events, putting on webinars, and maintaining social media accounts. If that sounds overwhelming, keep in mind that you do not need to be doing all of these things at once. Take your time and do each one in the best way you know how, consulting the brightest people at your disposal when conducting each campaign.

If you have the discipline to try each and every form of marketing that makes sense for your business, you will probably be surprised at two things: First, the number of things you thought would work which actually didn't, and second, that one or two methods you never thought would succeed, actually did. Two years ago, I advertised my marketing company in an industry newsletter, thinking it would come to little avail. After all, it was just one sentence about my business at the top of an email. It turns out that it brought more leads than any other campaign we had run since. If you try enough marketing channels, I guarantee you will have a similar story. I know it sounds expensive to do all that experimenting, but the successes pay for the failures. Plus, when buying advertising that is outside your usual comfort zone, you can always tell the salesperson that you want to start with a small "test buy" and will be happy to spend a lot more if it works. (Hey, it's true.) That will probably get you a deal.

Monetizing in Each Medium

Because every social media site and advertising channel has its own culture, I thought it would be helpful to briefly define each environment and describe how to reach customers.

- **Search engine ads**—People frequently use search engines when they are ready to make a purchase. Inside the search box, they are describing what they want to buy. The result they expect is a few lines of text with the *specific benefits* a seller can offer them. As a seller, your ad must address their search query with precision. For example, if someone is searching for "wedding proposal ideas" and they see an ad for a wedding planning company, it will not interest them; but an ad that offers to help them with their wedding *proposal* will work very well, because that is the specific subject of their query (see Figure 6.8).

> Wedding Proposal Planners
> Do you want a GREAT proposal to
> remember? We can plan it together.
> www.distinctiveproposals.com

Figure 6.8 *An example of a well-written search engine ad to respond to the query "wedding proposal ideas."*

- **Organic search results**—Whether or not your site already ranks highly for its main keywords, it must have a very clear path to the thing people are truly searching for. People don't search for a DUI lawyer because they are looking for information on the offense. They want to know what immediate steps they need to take to avoid embarrassment and jail time. Of the websites these searchers visit, the one that speaks to their true need quickest—and offers an appealing solution—gets them as a client.

- **Facebook ads**—People use social media to *socialize*, not to purchase things. They are happy to become part of a microcommunity of people with common interests, even one hosted by a seller (i.e. the seller's business page), as long as the community feels organic and not like an advertisement. As the person aiming to gather people onto your business page, you should *soft sell* entrance to this community by writing interesting ad copy that promises an interesting, educational social experience. If your ads feel friendly and not like a sales pitch, they will receive far more clicks (see Figure 6.9).

Figure 6.9 *An example of a well-written Facebook ad, which makes users feel like they are joining a social community rather than an advertising environment.*

- **Facebook personal profiles**—Facebook users are there to connect with their friends. Most won't connect with anyone they're not really friends with. However, you can still use your personal profile to target new customers. To do so, start adding people you have something in common with, either by grace of the fact that you have mutual friends or because they are an ideal customer. Know that most people won't accept, and do not send more than 5–8 friend requests per day. Start by adding all your real friends, as doing so will give you fewer degrees of separation from each potential customer you approach. This might also make you mutual friends with people to whom you want to sell. Make sure you include a personal message with the friend request indicating that the purpose is to form a relationship (see Figure 6.10). If you say anything impersonal or salesy, you will guarantee a rejection and may even get reported as spam. But if you request enough people over time, you will gain a foundation of new friends who will see your status updates and may become curious about what you do for a living if you are subtle enough with your status updates.

"If you say anything impersonal or salesy, you will guarantee a rejection and may even get reported as spam."

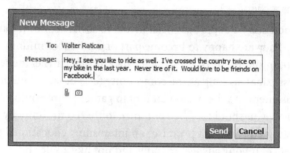

Figure 6.10 *If you were a motorcycle business owner, this is the kind of personal message you would want to attach to a friend request on Facebook to increase your chances of getting the request accepted.*

- **Twitter**—Twitter is a very good way to reach influential people in your field. It's the most egotistical of all the social media sites, which is perhaps why tastemakers love it. You acquire customers from Twitter mostly by having people with active followings tweet about your company. To get these tweets, email popular Twitter users in your industry or in the media and tell them, sincerely, about your company. Some small percentage will agree to do it. You can also offer to sponsor a tweet, which is less appealing to customers than an unpaid tweet but is a surer bet to get your message out there.

- **Niche website ads**—Advertising on a website where your target audience is already congregated is a tempting idea, and most niche sites will accept your money for an ad. This simple arrangement could be the most effective advertising you do. However, you need to understand how people use this website first so that your ad feels native to the site. For instance, if you were interested in advertising on TechCrunch, you should know that people read TechCrunch to learn what's going on in the tech and start-up worlds. Any ad you run on the site should be informational: mentioning an important person who joined your firm, a new patent you just secured, or a significant milestone your company hit. You would not say something like, "Get the best price on servers here!" as it would clash with the kind of editorial content people come to TechCrunch to read.

- **Forums**—Forums have been around about as long as the Internet. Yet, they still host some of the best, most specific discussions about various industry topics. If you focus on the right forums, you may find a group of serious potential customers who are there to learn about the field. Keep your eye on "marketplace"-type forums, and when you have time, dispense some of your knowledge. By becoming a known expert on the forum and leaving your website in your signature, you may get some incoming sales inquiries. You can also message people privately and offer them your services if their posts indicate a need.

- **Craigslist**—Most people find themselves on Craigslist at some point, either when looking for services in a business capacity or when searching for deals on items they desire. If you are in a business that sells something people seek out on Craigslist, post some ads. You'd be surprised at the level of sophistication—and budget—Craigslist users possess. When posting ads, make sure to showcase what makes your offering superior to others' and link to your website. Because there will likely be lots of ads from competitors, emphasize the *benefits* of your offering rather than the product or service itself.

- **Review sites**—If you are in a service industry, such as restaurants, nightlife, or travel, there are no words for how influential Yelp, Travelocity and other review sites can be. Good reviews can drive huge traffic. Do everything within your power to get good reviews from people who have done business with you. Message your customer base through your social media channels and remind them that reviews matter, and respond to every compliment (in-person or electronic) with a polite ask for a review.

- **Email**—Utilizing an email list is a proven way to convert customers. Building up the list is the toughest part of the equation. You do not want to buy lists, because most people don't respond kindly to unsolicited emails. One of the best ways to gain your own subscribers is by offering people something free and instantly retrievable in exchange for their email addresses, such as an e book, proprietary tool, or report. You can advertise your offer on industry websites, AdWords, or Facebook, as well as your own website. When describing your free offering, make sure it sounds both relevant and enticing. For instance, if you are an electrician, you might offer a paper called "Five Things You Definitely Don't Know About Hiring an Electrician." When emailing your list, it is important to provide examples of how people are using your product/service to its fullest benefit. If it's financial advising, for example, show how clients are making money; if it's knives, show how customers are slicing and dicing better. Straight sales letters do not work.

- **LinkedIn**—LinkedIn is the Facebook of business. It's different from Facebook in that it focuses on where people work, as well as their employment history and skills. Many people add all their business contacts to LinkedIn, and you should do the same. You will be impressed by the number of potential customers or business development partners one or two degrees away from your current contacts. Whenever there is a person or company I really want to speak with, the first thing I do is go to LinkedIn to see which of the people I know already has a relationship with them. Then I simply ask my connection to introduce me. You can also directly introduce yourself to people on LinkedIn, and they may add you to their network. Another benefit of LinkedIn is that it tells you how many connections people have on the service, which can be an indication of who the valuable connectors (tastemakers) in your industry might be.

- **Affiliate or direct referral relationships**—If you offer a really great service or product, you should approach business owners in a related industry and see if there is a fit. Many webmasters, bloggers, and speakers make substantial money recommending products they like and have a financial interest in. (A typical arrangement might be that if a sale results from an affiliate, the affiliate receives 30% of the gross revenues. Naturally, splits can vary widely.) If people really believe in your product or service, they may also send you business for no financial interest, just to help their clients.

- **Meetup.com**—There are few websites that facilitate real-world interactions anywhere near as effectively as Meetup.com. The site is simple to use: either join one of the hundreds of groups already on the site, or start your own around any topic. Starting a group that would appeal to your target demographic can be a brilliant business move. If you sell sports cars, for instance, you could start a group called Sports Car Lovers. If you get even 10 or 15 people at each meetup, that is 10 or 15 potential customers right in front of you.

- **Networking**—The key to networking is genuine passion. If you are excited about what you're doing and relate it in the form of a story rather than a pitch, people will feel it, and that feeling will translate to profits. I would argue that, for most businesses, a great networker is more important than a great Internet marketer. In-person relationships lead to far more referrals than any other sales medium. When you're out at conferences, events, or parties, you should be looking for people who will advocate for your business in some way—either through their influence, energy, or both. Influence and energy are equally valuable in a brand advocate. We all want Oprah to fiercely champion our business, but in reality, what we should be shooting for are people who know other people who also care a lot about our business.

Ultimately, social media is all about capturing attention. Your company's various social pages are not just competing with other social pages, but with every web page on the Internet; and its Internet presence is not just competing with other Internet presences, but with all the activities in which human beings participate. If you can make your pages useful or interesting enough to attract some of that attention, you are halfway toward monetization. The other half is selling something that people will buy, and then asking for payment in a simple, direct way. Selling through social media is just a more evolved version of classic mom-and-pop sales principles: be useful to your visitors, and they will reward you with their business.

7

The Possibilities of Social Data

This chapter is about the what-ifs and the what-will-be's. It is different from the other chapters in this book in that it does not offer practical tips that you can put into action today. However, its true use—and for the most entrepreneurial among you, this will be the most exciting use of all—is helping you to understand what our reality will look like in the next 5 to 10 years.

The phase of the Internet we're currently in, which is all about using social data to experience the world in a more human way, is slowly giving way to the kind of future we've been seeing portrayed in the movies since the 1980s. Picture waking up in your bedroom to the sound of your phone's alarm clock ringing. But instead of that dreaded beep-beep, beep-beep, beep-beep, it's a random song from your playlist or the voice of your favorite movie star telling you to rise and shine. The time is 7:15 a.m., a bit later than usual because traffic conditions have been reported as mild. As you groggily feel around for your phone and fix your sleepy eyes on it, a series of images flash by, which both show and tell you what is going on right now in your world. The weather is sunny, clear, and 65. Today you have a jog at 7:45, followed by your first meeting at 9:30 a.m.

Your custom news feed begins to stream in, courtesy of CNN. You have subscribed to the hyperlocal, entertainment, and good news channels. The pleasant automated voice tells you that a dog went missing about half a mile from your home, so be on the lookout for Sparky; Angelina Jolie and Brad Pitt have had their fourteenth child; and strides are being made in the water cleanliness of an important river in Tanzania.

Next comes your friend news feed, courtesy of Facebook. Sometimes you skip this part; other times you leave it on while you are showering. Three of your friends from Toronto are in town today, Adam went skydiving this past weekend and had a blast, Eunice got a new job, and Angela is mad because she's stuck in traffic. Oh, and don't forget—it's your cousin Jim's birthday today.

After you've gotten yourself out of the house and into the car, you instinctively plug in your phone to its port to continue receiving your personalized stream. Sometimes you listen to music, but today you feel like listening to the latest news from your industry, courtesy of Twitter. You are subscribed to the hashtag #design and tune into the newest design-related news, as curated by the people you follow.

Fifteen minutes later, it turns out it's your turn to hit traffic, but Google's step-by-step navigation kicks in, giving you an alternative route and even offering you a free coffee if you stop at the Starbucks along the way.

At work, you have a fairly routine day, except for the strange computer glitch that keeps slowing down your computer and making it more difficult for you to complete your work. Luckily, your phone is synced with your work computer and detects this error without any action on your part, comparing it with 1,874 similar cases that have occurred in the past 48 hours. It finds the best solution as voted by a community of tech-savvy people and automatically displays the solution on its screen, which allows you to resume productivity fairly quickly.

On the way home, your phone asks you if you are interested in the *American Idol Greatest Hits* album, which 12 of your friends have recently purchased. You decline. It then asks you if you are interested in traveling to Hawaii, because 38 of your friends have had positive experiences there. You're not sure if time and money will allow the trip, but you decide to listen in. Google analyzes the travel preferences you've inputted to TripAdvisor and Fodor's in the past two years and decides that you would be best off at the Westin in Kauai. The hotel rated an average of 4.5 stars from 400 people similar to you. As it turns out, Expedia can find you a flight there for only $499 round-trip, and there is even a daily deal on a massage at the hotel. Google Calendar informs you that you have a light schedule the week of May 4, and that would be the ideal time to travel. If you're interested in booking the trip, you're only a voice command and a security code confirmation away from having every aspect of the trip fully booked for you. You tell it to save the itinerary for another time.

Back at home, you start thinking about ordering dinner. Bringing up the Yelp app, you discover with one click which restaurants are delivering right now, and listen to a list of the top-rated ones based on your friends' preferences. Dinner is ordered and paid for through a few button pushes on the phone.

Now, what to do tonight? An app on your phone immediately informs you that two of your favorite movies are on TV, and then suggests a few other programs that it believes you'll like. Your Facebook app tells you which of your friends are listed as available tonight and of those, which are currently in your area. Separately, your phone gives you a list of 15 interesting people who have similar interests to your own who are hanging out at coffee shops, bars, and lounges nearby. Hang out with your current friends or make some new ones? Ah, decisions! As you get ready to go out, still undecided about what to do, you think to yourself "Man, I wish technology would be more helpful."

The Pandora of People

To me, the most exciting part of the previous scenario is the idea of "similar people"—not just getting recommendations from them, but meeting them. I've long pondered the fact that there are thousands of people I would probably love to know if only I could find them. And yet, the world is just too big. At best, we'll meet .0001% of its occupants in our lifetime. What's worse is that we spend so much time with people who aren't suited to us when that same time could be spent with people whom we truly relate to. If only there was some way to locate these folks!

I believe this technology is coming, and I call it the Pandora of People (or PoP for short). Recall that Pandora is a music prediction service that starts by asking you to input a song you like; it then builds a playlist of other songs it believes you'll like. The accuracy of its recommendations is striking, and millions of people have discovered new music they never would have heard if not for Pandora.

A Pandora of People would operate very similarly: you type the name of one of your friends into the search box and the program recognizes the person, bringing up a detailed profile of their likes, interests, and personality characteristics. It then queries its database, comparing this friend to hundreds of thousands of other people living within, say, 50 miles of you. In addition, it compares each potential "similar person" to its profile of you. The result is a list of perhaps 100 people whom you ought to meet.

Although this hypothetical program sounds a lot like a dating website's algorithm, it is quite different for two main reasons: First, the quantity of data that the program would have about you is much greater than on any dating site because it incorporates years of online social interaction and preference inputting, learning from not only what you tell it but from what you actually do; second, the number of people it has to compare is much larger, because far more people have a social profile than a dating profile. The fact that the social profile would have been created for online socializing rather than dating also makes a difference because the information on it is likely to be more casual and honest—and therefore, more reliable. Think of it as Facebook friend suggestions on steroids.

For any company to do a PoP well, they would need access to a long-standing social profile and an ingenious algorithm. The answer to the first need is, of course, Facebook. The answer to the second may lie in applying a psychologically based approach to the rubric of Pandora's algorithm.

Pandora's music discovery engine analyzes a number of factors about your starting song, including the pacing (bpm), the type of instruments used, the melodic composition, and even the timbre of the lead singer's voice. Similarly, the PoP would need to analyze the core elements of a potential friend's personality as well as the factors that make two people compatible.

Finding similarities between people, such as their taste in music, movies, or food, or the types of activities they enjoy, could be accomplished fairly easily using Facebook's extensive data set. However, determining true compatibility would require a deeper dive into the data pool. It is my contention that most successful relationships—whether platonic or romantic—exist between people who feel a similar comfort with themselves. Although the emotional strengths of both people may vary widely (one may excel at talking about feelings, the other at being self-confident), the magnitude of comfort with each person's self is usually about equal in a good relationship. This quality, complex as it may seem, could be determined to some degree using Facebook. For instance, people who frequently post self-reflective status updates probably have more in common than people who often post utilitarian status updates about things or places. Although your Facebook status updates can't conclusively measure how comfortable you are with yourself, I believe there is a correlation. In my own life, certainly, many of the people I get along with best write status updates that relate to personal growth just as I do.

A few key background items also impact compatibility significantly—perhaps more so than any other factors. Among them: where you were raised, religion, and age.

All told, I am willing to bet that if a script were to produce a group of people that post status updates similar in emotional depth to mine; who like some of my favorite movies, books, music, and food; who share my religion and general area where I grew up; and are within five years of my age, there would be some great new friends among them. I would guess there are at least 100 people that fit those criteria, and eliminating certain factors that aren't as important to me, such as religion, would expand that group even further.

Someone invent this thing please! (Zuckerberg, you know how to reach me.)

Figure 7.1 shows a mock-up of how a "Pandora of People" might work.

Figure 7.1   *An illustration of how a Pandora of People might look.*

However, the object of the Pandora of People is not just friendship; it is mining social recommendations as well. As I've mentioned, Google already employs a "similar people" algorithm to recommend local places to Google users (see Figure 7.2). But that kind of usage is only the beginning. If the "similar people" algorithm is robust enough that the people in the resultset are truly similar (at least in one category, such as movies or travel), it could be used to recommend thousands of products and services to people over their lifetimes, which would create a powerful revenue model for whomever owns that algorithm.

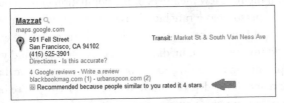

Figure 7.2   *The earliest form of the "similar to you" concept at work from September 2011. In this case, Google is using the tastes of a similar pool of people to recommend a restaurant.*

In fact, Facebook is currently swimming in the stream of revenue coming from comparing people's tastes, known to us as *social discovery*. And Google is desperate to catch up. For Google, it would be a dream to not only be the engine that delivers people to the products they *know* they want—for that is essentially what Google already does—but also to recommend *new* products that they are likely to buy. At the present time, only Facebook has enough social data to have a shot at selling people things they didn't know they wanted just because others like those things. We will see how Google does with its social strategy—or whether consumers ever decide to untether from Facebook and demand a portable social profile that can be uploaded to any website to personalize the experience. For now, we can all watch as Facebook attempts to utilize the depth and breadth of its data without alienating users because of privacy concerns.

Social Data As a Life Saver

The obvious categories for social search and discovery to embrace are entertainment, travel, food, and shopping. That is because people are most comfortable being public about these kinds of things. It's fun to show your friends the city you just landed in, the unique cuisine you're eating, and the new gadget you just bought. And doing so will feed the social data monster, who will eventually spit out recommendations personalized just for you. But have you ever thought of sharing information about the doctor you saw, the job interview you had, or the bad date you went on? Believe it or not, these hitherto off-limits categories will eventually get the light of social data shined on them. (Indeed, Yelp already features ratings of doctors and pretty much every other service provider.) Could social data find you a romantic partner? I think we can all imagine so. But could it save your life? Now that's an interesting proposition.

Here's how I get to social data saving your life: A few years from now, we're all sharing our tastes and preferences on social media channels more than ever. We routinely rate our doctors, describe their strengths and weaknesses, and report our experiences with them. A few members of the population end up having unique experiences. One person has a rare blood disease and decides to attempt an experimental surgery that is being conducted in Europe. It saves his life and he shares it with the world through social media. A few years later, *you* find yourself in a similarly compromising position, and although you've never heard of this person, you search the name of the disease and find his story. Now you're on your way to Europe and you, too, are given a new lease on life because of the information that was assembled for you in the new world of social data. That is just one example.

In the future, most people will take advantage of social media's application to the medical field in a more mundane way. Looking for an internist to give you a general checkup? Wouldn't it be great to be able to go to Google, Facebook, Bing, or some third-party application using social data and filter the millions of available doctors down to just the ones located in your city who participate in your health insurance plan and have earned an average of 5 out of 5 stars from your social connections (see Figure 7.3)? Although some medical sites out there may claim to have this technology already, our social graph today is not meaty enough for this approach to work; that is, not enough people have rated their doctors to create a pool of social data that can be truly relied upon.

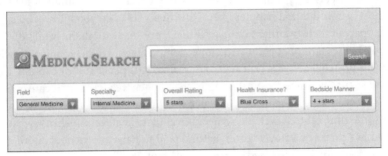

Figure 7.3 *A theoretical medical search engine that takes social data into account.*

Another important application of social data will be in the area of jobs. We can all imagine an improved version of the type of referral-based job hunting that LinkedIn currently facilitates. That is, instead of searching LinkedIn for the hiring manager of a certain company and then working your way through your connections to contact this person, you could start with a menu of all your friends' jobs, broken down by field, availability of positions, and location—as well as some juicier features, such as salary, benefits, and job satisfaction level.

An even more exciting use of social data is helping people to understand what kind of job is right for them. Before getting into how such a process would work, let me say that I am of the belief that loving what you do is paramount. After all, even if you put quality-of-life considerations aside, people who are genuinely engaged in their work tend to be more productive and make more money. And because work tends to take up 40 or more hours per week, it's crucial to find the right career. Like most people, I had no idea what I wanted to do until long after college, when I was thrown into something I happened to enjoy. I then spent years doing things that gave me some satisfaction, but still weren't ideal for me. Doing what I truly love—writing, speaking, and developing cutting-edge marketing strategies—took me eight years.

I imagine a program, fueled by social data, that helps people figure out what they want to do for a living as soon as they're ready to work. It relies on the openness of online sharing that will define the coming age, an openness that has been led by Facebook and Twitter. As people begin to share more about their jobs—day-to-day responsibilities, hours, and educational requirements, as well as salaries, benefits, and job satisfaction (anonymously, of course)—a new age of career searching will be upon us. We will have the luxury of seeing which jobs have the most satisfaction overall, the highest ratio of satisfaction to pay, and other creative scenarios such as highest salary/fewest hours and highest salary/lowest required education. Even more significantly, however, we will be able to see what kind of jobs *people like us* ended up loving.

If all of us, especially youth, had a way to know which careers would nourish us the most, we would lead happier lives. How many folks do you know who spent a good part of their twenties taking jobs that were "beneath them" while they waited for the right opportunity to come along? Imagine if the young man who spent his postcollege years waiting tables realized his penchant for cooking early on and spent that same time dabbling in the kitchen, readying for a career as a chef. Or that young woman who interned at a literary agency for a while and then took some time off to travel and write a novel that she never finished—what if she started her career as a travel writer, getting paid to have experiences in other countries, and eventually published a great novel about it? The fantasy of holding your dream job will be closer to a reality before we know it, given the right equation of entrepreneurial ingenuity and mass participation in social media.

The Inner Workings of "People Similar to You"

The beginnings of this socially-driven future are taking place at Google and Facebook, as well as the thousands of smaller app companies that study social data. At the center of this bubbling cauldron of development are two crucial questions. The first is, "Who matters to you?" We covered that subject in Chapter 2, "The New Influences in Search and Social Media," when we discussed tastemakers and Google and Facebook's desperate quest to figure out whose opinion you trust the most in each category of life. The second question is, "Who is similar to you?" An algorithm that accurately matches up people with common characteristics is the holy grail among the big tech companies, because it essentially breaks us loose from the closed circle of friends we currently belong to, exposing the vast universe of connections beyond it. The difference between today's social media and a social media with a working "people similar to you" algorithm is like the difference between your music library and your music library powered by Pandora: one simply stores all your favorite songs, whereas the other constantly exposes you

> "An algorithm that accurately matches up people with common characteristics is the holy grail among the big tech companies..."

to new songs. We need both. I believe that when you bring like-minded people into your life, a kind of magic happens. Suddenly you have not just your own life experiences guiding you, but others' as well, and you discover wonderful new things you didn't know existed.

So how do these "people similar to you" algorithms work? The first thing they do is look for people who like the same things. Google gets this information from three sources: your IP address (which indicates your location), your Google Places ratings and reviews, and your Google+ account, if you have one.

Google Places is the environment in which "people similar to you" was first tested on the public at large and, at the time of this writing, the only major site where the concept exists (although plenty of start-ups are toying with it). The algorithm behind it is probably pretty basic: if the majority of your top-rated dining establishments are high-end seafood restaurants, you become, for the purposes of the algorithm, a person who likes expensive fish. In this scenario, Google effectively captures two variables about you: cuisine choice and budget. In the travel realm, they can ascertain what type of vacation you prefer. Are you more of an outdoors lover, a luxury hotel stayer, or a family resort goer? Of course, shades of gray exist; perhaps you have some of each type in you. But in the end, Google now understands two additional variables—hotel choice and vacation type—while also gaining a better sense of your budget.

If you actively rate and review restaurants and travel experiences, Google already has a profile for you. Here is what such an early profile might look like:

IP Address: 192.68.233

Known names: James Darby, tigershark233

Lives in: New York, NY

Cuisine Preferences: Mexican—21%, Seafood—16%, Tapas—13%, Sandwiches—11%, Italian—8%, Indian—6%, French—6%, Sushi—5%, Chinese—5%, Mediterranean—4%, Ethiopian—3%, Vegetarian—2%

Food Budget: $—28%, $$—56%, $$$—10%, $$$$—6%

Vacation Preference: Camping—31%, Skiing—25%, Family—19%, Luxury—13%, Adventure—12%

Hotel Preference: *—0%, **—5% ***—45% ****—35% *****—15%

In the future, these profiles will become a lot richer and the algorithm far more sophisticated. Google will start to cull bits and pieces of your reviews, especially sentences containing strong language, to get a better sense of what you care about. The kind of words that would resonate are "loved," "hated," "worst," "best," "incredible," and "awful." Learning what kind of nouns these adjective and verbs are referring to will complete the picture. Google can chalk up one "similarity point" to people that [verb] the same [nouns] or find the same [nouns] very [adjective]. This sort of machine learning is exactly what Google is best at.

Yet, we are still in such an early 2010s mindset with basic machine learning technology. Most likely, Google is already working hard to understand not just peoples' reactions to places but their core belief systems and opinions. As Google becomes more social as a company, it will use every bit of data it can get to classify people into complex groupings, somewhat like we've all read about in Psychology 101 but far more detailed. Whereas Myers-Briggs has the INFJ (Introverted Intuition with Extroverted Feeling), Google might have something like the intensely passionate, wholly optimistic, wryly funny, rock 'n' roll loving, sushi craving, New York living, Europe vacationing, reality TV watching, jeans wearing, technology reading, corporation distrusting, somnambulant hipster. Of course, all of this will be expressed in dense code.

Although I write some of the previous paragraph in jest, Google will have an understanding at least as rich as the one I described; in fact, it is likely that the company will classify people using hundreds of characteristics rather than just a handful.

As a marketer, how can you capitalize on an Internet that will heavily utilize a "people similar to you" algorithm? To begin with, you'll want to appear similar to a lot of people so that the maximum number of folks will have the things you like—including your own products and services—suggested to them. You could rate or like lots of things in order to be considered similar to more people, but this strategy is both tenuous and temporary. The most valuable course of action you can take is to become a tastemaker yourself so that your social connections see your recommendations, and to impel others, especially other tastemakers, to like what you're selling. In fact, I might call that strategy the central marketing conclusion of this book: In the new social landscape, the number and prominence of people who publicly like or share your product will determine how many people see it.

Corporate and Government Uses of Social Data

As we sit here today, insurance companies have already begun investigating ways to use social data to predict the risk of something happening to you. Why ask when you can see for yourself? If there are public pictures of you smoking, don't be surprised if your life insurance premium rises. If you list skateboarding as an interest on a public profile, you may find your health insurance costs on the rise.

The same very well might occur with banks and credit card companies. Signs of responsibility and irresponsibility will be gleaned from your social profiles to help round out your credit score or inform a decision to lend. So be careful if you tweet about buying things you can't afford or hating to pay your bills. Even seemingly mundane details like whether you are married and how long you've maintained a LinkedIn profile could demonstrate consistency in the eyes of a financial institution.

However, big institutions will not rely solely on social data. Their business model relies on making highly accurate predictions based on hard data. Most likely, the algorithms they use will continue to focus on more reliable data. In the case of insurance companies, that would mean medical diagnoses or hospital check-ins, and in the case of banks, that would mean payment history and available cash. But I fully expect a percentage of their algorithm to factor in the information you are announcing to the world.

Here are some other scenarios in which social data could creep into our experience with big institutions:

- A hotel could check your social influence using an online influence measurement tool or by looking at your number of friends, followers, fans, or connections, giving you perks if they determine you are a taste-maker.

- An online retailer could check the presence of your name and email address in a shared retailer database to ensure that you are a legitimate person with a public profile who regularly makes purchases.

- Marketing companies could target you with advertisements if you've publicly stated that you like or dislike certain products or services. (As we all know, this is Facebook's business model, but in this context I am referring to companies other than Facebook mining public data to target you by email, postal mail, or telephone.) If a company has just a few pieces of data on you, they can easily research you and infer what you might want to buy.

- A religious institution or other member-supported community might give preferential treatment to new members who are listed as donors on various websites.

There are hundreds more scenarios in which social data will be used to make better and faster decisions about us. In fact, it is easy to picture a world in the not-so-distant future where every person emanates data from their cell phone—locational, transactional, and emotional—that companies can use to create "heat maps" of sorts to understand local marketing environments better (see Figure 7.4). I can imagine maps that track marketing niches such as "openness to new experiences," "willingness to spend money," and "most engaged with brands." These kinds of maps would help to drive decisions about where to open up businesses, distribute flyers, and run location-based ad campaigns.

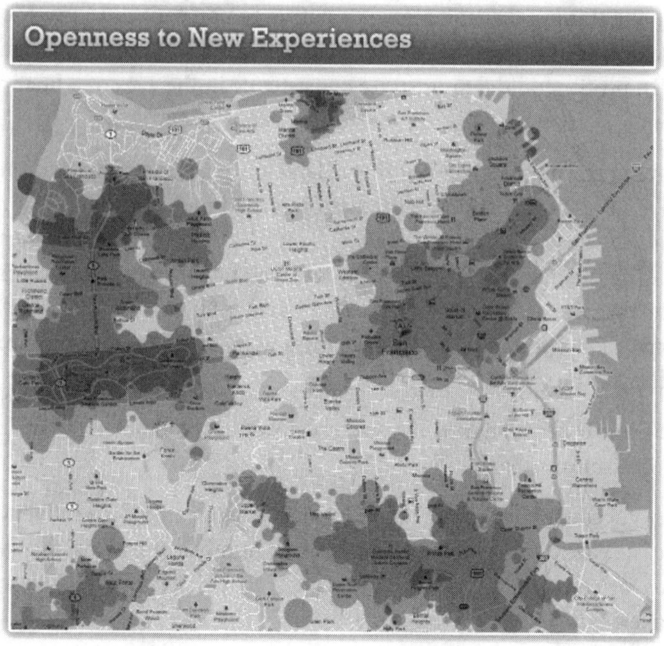

Figure 7.4 *Examples of the kind of "heat maps" that will be possible when social data is more widespread. This kind of information will aid corporations and marketers tremendously, while potentially infringing on consumers' privacy and quality of life.*

Although the specifics of how social data will ultimately be manifested are unknown right now, the notion that it will be an essential tool for corporations in the future is indisputable. The only variable that could slow down the data train is privacy. If legislation gets passed barring data collection companies from using our blog comments, forum posts, and status updates—including the ones we've erased—to analyze us, there will be less reason to watch everything we post. But as always, the sagest advice of all remains, "If you don't want the world to see it, don't put it online."

Putting aside unsettling corporate uses of social data, there are some markedly positive applications of social data as well. One of the best examples is in the realm of emergency response. Organizations dedicated to saving people's lives are using social data to understand the causes of accidents better and even to communicate with people in dire situations. The Red Cross has a blog dedicated specifically to the use of social media to provide immediate help. From one post:

> If web users knew of someone else who needed help, 44 percent would
> ask other people in their social network to contact authorities, 35 percent
> would post a request for help directly on a response agency's Facebook
> page, and 28 percent would send a direct Twitter message to responders.

If these numbers rise, which they inevitably will, social media will play an increasingly substantial role in emergency responses. It is already used widely in other governmental capacities, such as by police in investigations and by criminal courts as evidence.

I can imagine governments using social data in far more creative ways though. We all watched the uprisings in Egypt and Libya and the riots in London in 2011, which were fueled by social networks and cell phone chat programs. If the government were to monitor quality of life more carefully (and cared to do so), they might have been able to communicate better with the people and prevent bloodshed.

Governments might in the near future start monitoring social media for more mundane reasons: to get a sense of how constituents are living and feeling. After all, every social issue is discussed thoroughly online, and algorithms exist that can filter out extreme opinions on both sides of the spectrum. The result could be an accurate picture of what most people feel about a given issue. True measurement of public opinion would obviate the need for expensive polling and focus groups and give those in charge better insight into people's lives.

Facebook and the Future of Social Data

The future possibilities of social data have a lot to do with the preferences of the handful of people who control the biggest social networks. If Google, Facebook, and Twitter—leaving aside all of the smaller companies collecting valuable data—decided to share all their data, we the consumers would be exposed to all the possibilities of social data much quicker. But there is currently an attitude of extreme competition between the three major companies playing in the social space, and none of them want to relent.

Facebook shoulders most of the responsibility for the bottleneck of innovation in the social space, because it has many times more information than any other company and

"Facebook shoulders most of the responsibility for the bottleneck of innovation in the social space, because it has many times more information than any other company and is not particularly dedicated to sharing it."

is not particularly dedicated to sharing it. As a Facebook user, I have watched the website morph in ways large and small over the years, and at no point did I feel that the betterment of people's lives was a priority. Although it's true that Facebook keeps me updated on my friends' lives, it is more of a distraction than anything—and one that seems focused on revenue generation above all else. Whereas Google provides us with tools such as Google Earth, Google Maps, Gmail, and Chrome, Facebook keeps us glued to pictures of our high school crushes. Twitter also paints a stark contrast with Facebook, having been instrumental in the dissemination of news and current events and far less focused on revenue.

Although we can't fault Facebook for striving to be financially successful, there is a difference between innovating purely for profit and innovating for profit *and* social good. I think it would be wise for Facebook to use the incredible amount of social data it possesses to solve real problems for people. As the company begins to know enough about people to make predictions about them from an advertising stand-point, it would also make sense to help people find schools, jobs, doctors, pastimes, places to vacation, and new friends. I truly believe that evolving the usefulness of the Internet will earn them more money in the long term than jealously guarding their social data so that only they can profit from it. Let's not forget their stated mission: "Making the world more open and connected."

For the time being though, Facebook is what it is—a company focused on accruing social data in order to build the most valuable advertising product in the industry, supplanting Google Adwords. If we are to take advantage of its incredible pool of data, we must master Facebook Ads, and that is the subject of the next chapter.

8

Dominating Facebook Ads

Facebook ads are the culmination of the greatest human classification ever conducted. Using high-octane scripts, Facebook has found a way to slice and dice the population into every group and subgroup you can imagine. In the old days—that is, five years ago—companies had to go to websites to advertise to specific demographics. If you were a games company looking to advertise to 18–35-year-old males, you went to one of a few websites that served that niche. A makeup company aimed at tween females had about six choices if it wanted to reach a large audience, and each of those websites would likely charge much more than the average small business could afford. Today, any company can reach 13-year-old females living in major cities who like makeup, and do so for a tiny fraction of the price of an ad spend on a popular website. They can laser-target to demographics and psychographics in ways that marketers only dreamed of just a few years back.

Facebook Versus Google: The Battle for Your Purchasing Power

It's strange to realize that Facebook was second to the online advertising innovation party. Google created AdWords in 2002, and with it revolutionized the advertising industry by allowing companies to show ads to users in response to specific searches. This meant that advertisers no longer had to wonder if the people viewing their ads were interested in their product. They could literally show ads only to people searching for exactly what they sell. That is a powerful proposition, and the reason why Google is a far larger company than Facebook at present.

> "...as I've mentioned many times in this book, Google is scared. The biggest threat to its AdWords product—by far— is Facebook ads.

But, as I've mentioned many times in this book, Google is scared. The biggest threat to its AdWords product—by far—is Facebook ads. That is because Google simply cannot target as specifically as Facebook can. In the previous example of the tween girl makeup company, which ad product would make more sense for them? Let's consider AdWords first. If a tween girl is looking for makeup, what exactly would she search for on Google? "tween girl makeup"? I don't think so. Probably something like "buy makeup," which puts her into a pool of tens of thousands of other searchers of all ages. More likely, she wouldn't search for anything on Google and would instead navigate to her favorite makeup site.

Now let's consider Facebook Ads. We know that young girls are on Facebook—most of them, actually. And many of them have already publicly stated that they like certain makeup brands. The company in question could run a campaign that shows ads to girls of a specific age who like Sephora. That is a much more targeted offering than anything Google has right now.

The rub, of course, is that these young girls who like makeup—the ideal demographic and psychographic for the example company—are not necessarily looking for makeup at the moment. If people used Facebook as a shopping search engine the way they do Google, Facebook would have it made. The moment these girls start looking for makeup, they could see ads from the makeup company. But alas, Google is still the place people go to search.

As you can see, a perfect complement exists between online socialization and search. The company that is best at social can deliver *exactly* the right group of people to advertisers. But the company that is best at search can deliver purchases. You would think that Google and Facebook would be dying to combine resources so that they could both make mountains of money.

But Facebook won't have it. I place the onus on Facebook because the attitude at Google right now is, "We're the good guys—we just want to work with the other social networks," whereas the attitude at Facebook is, "We're pretty sure that we're on the precipice of taking over the world."

If I could bring you back to a familiar Wild West analogy for a moment, the companies are like two saloons situated next to each other. One of them has the best liquor—but no glasses. And the other has exquisite glasses—but no liquor. It would only make sense for the two operations to combine, but the one with the glasses is pretty sure it can make its own liquor. The one with the liquor, on the other hand, is quite eager to borrow glasses from its neighbor; but upon being repeatedly rejected, it has been forced to make glasses itself. The problem is, glassmaking is not its strength and its glasses are shoddy and difficult to drink from. Meanwhile, the other bar is beginning to produce its own liquor, and while everyone agrees that the neighbor's liquor is far superior, they figure hey, at least it's a way to have a drink.

In case it's not clear, Facebook is that overconfident saloon with the exquisite glasses that would rather make its own liquor—the liquor being purchasing power—than share its precious glasses (the glasses being targeted advertising groups). Google has tried again and again to borrow Facebook's targeted advertising groups in exchange for giving it a share of the purchasing power, but Facebook refuses to budge, confident that it will eventually get people to start using Facebook to make purchases. And so Google is forced to make its own vessels for classifying people. Currently, that effort is called Google+. But there is something unnatural about it.

Figure 8.1 illustrates how Facebook feels that its superior targeting ability will lead to more consumer purchases over time than Google has. Thus, Facebook is not willing to share its social data. Google currently has much more influence over consumers' purchases; but if Facebook has its way, that situation will soon change.

Figure 8.1   *This cartoon illustrates Facebook's attitude toward Google as a competitor.*

So what truth is there to Facebook's hunch? Can it really become the advertising force that leaves Google in the dust? Well, there *is* something to it. Facebook users are willing to search on Facebook, whereas Google users are not particularly willing to socialize on Google. (We will see if that situation changes as Google+ evolves.) Facebook users currently perform over a billion searches per month into the little white box at the top of every page, so there is clearly a comfort searching on Facebook. The leap to searching for keywords rather than people or pages would be a large one, but if there was some way for Facebook to return only search results that friends or people similar to you like, and keep people within the Facebook ecosystem after they perform a search, a very interesting situation could occur. It's all a matter of inventing the first truly useful social search on the Web.

Ultimately, both companies are gunning to gain insight on every facet of people's lives so that they can understand, almost down to the hour, how people are living. Whoever can get closest to knowing how people feel at any given time of day will have tapped into a new realm of advertising. The ultimate form of advertising, after all, is thought-reading ads: messages that respond to a craving for salty foods with an ad for potato chips, or a feeling of romantic longing with an ad for a dating website, or a state of anxiety with an ad for a massage. The closer Facebook and Google get to that advertising nirvana, the more appealing their platforms will become.

How to Think About Facebook Ads

It is easy to see how Facebook is such a threat to Google and other advertising-driven businesses. Their ads are beginning to show real promise. Whereas as late as 2010, there were few solid case studies about the effectiveness of Facebook ads, by 2011 hundreds of case studies showed Facebook ads driving sales. If you haven't tried Facebook ads—or more likely, tried it and found it to be ineffective—you absolutely *need* to know a couple of basic things before investing further in the Facebook ads platform.

First, you should know which industries are right for Facebook ads versus Google ads. If you are an e-commerce website selling specific products, Google AdWords is probably a better platform for you. But if you are an event producer trying to sell tickets, you want to be advertising on Facebook.

One easy way to decide which platform to use is to ask yourself, "Do people go to Google to find my product?" If so, AdWords is your man. But if people aren't specifically seeking out what you sell, Facebook makes more sense. Another test is to ask whether your product is in any way involved in people's social lives. If it's a local place, or a member of the beauty, lifestyle, restaurant, or entertainment industries, for instance, Facebook ads are worth investing in.

Take a look at the following chart for some guidance on which industries are best suited for Facebook versus Google.

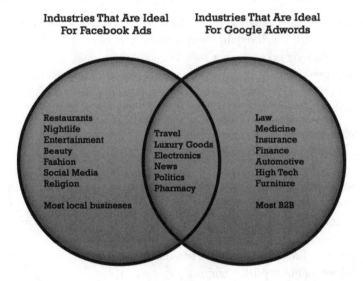

Figure 8.2 *Some industries are better fits for Facebook, some for Google, and some are good fits for both ad platforms.*

Most Facebook ads are little rectangles that appear on the side of the page. (Another type of ad, introduced in January 2012, is called a "Sponsored Story," and appears inside your News Feed just like a status update.) I have already outlined the basics of setting up a Facebook ad campaign in Chapter 2, "The New Influences in Search and Social Media." Assuming you now understand how to do that, I'd like to take a deeper dive into how you should be viewing your Facebook ad campaigns.

Ideally, before running any Facebook ads, every person should take a Psychology 101 class. The key to success with this platform is understanding what different groups of people are intrigued by. If you can do that, more people will click your ad, and Facebook rewards highly clicked ads by making them less expensive. In other words, you are doubly incentivized to get people interested in your ads.

When my company first started offering Facebook fan-building services, we simply created relevant ads for each client until we found a few that people consistently clicked. Now we have the process down to a science, with a team of people scoring words, phrases, and images by emotional resonance. But even as we address the process scientifically, we also treat each finished ad like a piece of art. And all art begins with a blank canvas.

The shape of the ad's canvas is approximately 280 pixels wide by 130 pixels tall, with an image inside of it that is no larger than 110 by 80 pixels. The text of the ad may be up to 135 characters long, with the title limited to 25 characters. Those are your borders. But what happens within those borders is pretty much infinite.

If you think of Facebook ads as merely a system for gaining new customers (a boring one at that, which requires setting up ad after ad in order to find a usable one), you will never become a maestro. You need to be looking at Facebook ads as a unique expression of creativity—one that has a much greater monetary reward than most other creative endeavors. Facebook ads can actually be fun if you turn them into a personal challenge.

My brother Brad and I create Facebook ads all the time, and we like to figure out ways to make them more interesting. He often places my image in ads for the events we produce, saying slightly ridiculous things about me. For example, we have competitions where we see who can create the most successful ad involving a picture of an animal. Sometimes the usual fare—pictures of adorable puppies or kittens accompanied by a request to like a page ("Click Like! It will make Rover happy.")—works beautifully. But other times, we need to verge on the idiosyncratic. Figure 8.3 shows an ad that got an incredible click-through rate and won lots of respect in our brotherly competition.

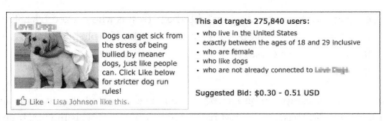

Figure 8.3 *A Facebook ad my company used to promote a conference I was speaking at. The conference website has been intentionally blurred.*

The formula for an ad that "goes viral"—gets such a high click-through rate that the cost per like is mere pennies—is part experience, part inspiration, and part luck. I will get to that in a minute. Let me back up a second, though, and explain the terms that I used in the past few paragraphs.

There are five main advertising terms you need to know in relation to online ads: impression, click-through rate, cost per click, and cost per thousand impressions. For Facebook ads specifically, the term "cost per like" is particularly important. If you already know these terms, then zoom right by this section. You won't miss anything.

- **Impression**—An instance of an ad appearing on someone's screen, whether they saw it or not. If you've heard the term "page view," an impression is basically the same thing.

- **Click-through rate (CTR)**—The percentage of ads that got clicked on out of all the times the ads were shown to users. If an ad got 100 impressions and was clicked on three times, it would have a 3% CTR.

- **Cost per click (CPC)**—A popular way that ad companies charge for advertising, which requires you to pay a certain amount every time one of your ads is clicked. If your CPC is $0.50, you are paying 50 cents every time a user clicks your ad.

- **Cost per thousand impressions (CPM)**—Another popular way that ad companies charge for advertising, which requires you to pay a certain amount for every thousand impressions your ad receives. If your CPM is $1, you are paying one dollar every time your ad is shown 1,000 times. One thousand ad appearances, or impressions, does not mean that 1,000 different people saw the ad. It could mean that the ad was seen 1,000 times by 1 person, or 50 times by 20 people.

- **Cost per like (CPL)**—This term is not officially used by Facebook, but it is the most convenient way of evaluating Facebook ads when you are trying to build a fan base. It refers to the cost you pay, whether by CPC or CPM, to acquire one Like on your page. The quality of the Like can vary wildly, depending on who the person is who clicked Like. The CPL for a 60-year-old doctor from Los Angeles is probably going to be far more expensive than that of a 15-year-old student from a developing country.

When running a campaign on Facebook, you have a choice between running your ads on a CPC basis or a CPM basis. For beginners, CPC is the better choice, because you can feel assured that you are paying only when some level of interest has been expressed in your ad. Facebook gives CPC-based ads special attention, showing them higher up in the advertising column than CPM ads, and not showing them at all if there is a low likelihood of an interested party clicking them. In contrast, CPM ads are always shown if you bid beyond a certain level, belying an attitude on Facebook's part of, "We'll show 'em, but we don't guarantee people will care about 'em." For this reason, CPM advertising is best for building a base of supporters, whereas if it's purely buyers you are looking for, CPC is the way to go.

The reason CPC advertising is generally a better choice is as simple as the fact that Facebook has a guarantee of revenue for each click. CPM prices generally tend to be lower, and as such, Facebook gives them inferior placement, which usually results in lower-quality fans.

 Note

Although these statements about CPC versus CPM advertising are commonly held, and certainly encapsulate my own experience, they are not always true. Facebook is constantly tinkering with its ad system, and there are always outlying cases where CPM campaigns outperform CPC campaigns for some unexplainable reason. So it is always wise to do your own testing with both styles of advertising.

At this point, you should be getting the feeling that the amount you are willing to pay determines the performance of your ads. This is generally true, because Facebook is a for-profit corporation. However, there is an aspect of Facebook ads that is still in its Wild West phase.

As I've already explained, you have the opportunity to pay significantly

> "...you should be getting the feeling that the amount you are willing to pay determines the performance of your ads."

less money if your ads perform well—that is, get a very high click-through rate. If you can consistently create high-CTR ads, you will have "beat the system," and can pay a fraction of the price that others are paying for the same quality clicks. There is just one rub, though, and that's that Facebook "corrects" high-performing campaigns after a certain length of time. Simply put, if your ads are performing especially well, delivering tons of likes at a very low CPL, a person or algorithm at Facebook will break up the party at some point. Every great ad has its moment, and that moment doesn't ever last more than two days.

Facebook maintains what some call a "house price," which is the amount it *wants* you to pay for your advertising campaign. This rate is determined by comparing what another advertiser would pay if they occupied your same spot. For that reason, ads targeted to valuable Facebook groups—CEOs, for instance—are particularly expensive, not because of a higher perceived value on Facebook's part, but because so many other people would gladly pay a handsome amount to reach that group. For example, if you create an ad that appeals tremendously to CEOs, temporarily acquiring likes from them at $.05 per like, your CPL will soon rise dramatically as Facebook realizes that it could get much more from other advertisers.

The existence of this "house price" is the reason that, if you really want to master Facebook ads, you need to be able to write great ads constantly. If you've never created a high-CTR ad (also known as a "viral ad"), this may sound like a pipe dream to you; but it is very much a learnable skill that comes with practice. However, like all good Wild Wests, I predict that viral ads will become a thing of the past at some point—probably within two years of the publication of this book. So while you have the opportunity, practice this skill. Facebook fan bases will be no less valuable when the price to acquire them skyrockets.

As a point of comparison, Google AdWords used to be a Wild West. I remember the days when you could run an AdWords campaign and acquire a valuable visitor to your website for 10 cents. That was back in 2005. Within a few years, Google's "house price" for most types of ads had jumped dramatically, escalating in waves. Today, there are few industries where Google AdWords clicks can be snagged for a song. (That is why I always advise clients to use AdWords only if the product or service they sell is fairly expensive—$100 or more per item. Even then, it can take months to optimize your ads and landing page so that Google will give you a reasonable price per click on a regular basis.)

> "I always advise clients to use AdWords only if the product or service they sell is fairly expensive—$100 or more per item."

The 10 Commandments of Amazing Facebook Ads

So, how does one create a "viral ad," you ask? Why, by following the 10 Commandments of Amazing Facebook Ads....

When you have fully implemented these rules, you should begin to notice your ads doing significantly better than before. This does not mean that every ad will get an incredible click-through rate. You'll figure out which ads work best for your target group over the course of running dozens of ads. My hope, though, is that this list will give you the proper perspective from which to view your ads so you're not just shooting in the dark.

And when you *do* start knocking it out of the park on your CTR, remember that clicks and even phenomenally low ad prices do not equal revenue. It is exciting to acquire fans inexpensively, but the only thing that matters at the end of the day is your ROI. So even if you get fans at $1 a fan, if you can average $1.50 in revenue for each of those fans, you've succeeded in successfully marketing on Facebook.

Thy Picture Must Be Relevant

Advertising to an ecotourism crowd? Don't show a picture of a smiling baby. Show a picture of a smiling frog instead. In addition to relevance, familiarity is also important. People are more likely to click on a logo they're already familiar with than a brand-new one, and the same is true with all images. In the case of the ecotourism-targeted ad, you would want to show chinchilla lovers pictures of chinchillas, and kangaroo lovers pictures of kangaroos. Sounds obvious, but it can't be emphasized enough.

Thy Call to Action Must Be Clear

From their earliest days, people are trained to obey. So giving clear orders, as long as they're said in a friendly context, is a great way to increase likelihood that your ad will be clicked. I've found that calls to action either at the beginning or the end of an ad work best. A beginning-of-ad call to action might say something like, "Click here if you think Justin Bieber should be president" (I'm sorry) or "Click Like if you feel orangutans ought to be protected." An end-of-ad call to action might be "Click to join the movement!"

Honor Thy Fans' Complementary Interests

It is tempting to target your ad by the exact interests your company caters to. For instance, if you own a nightclub, you might want to target your ads to people who like nightclubs and lounges. However, expanding your psychographic (interest group) can produce fans who are even more energized than the members of your original target audience. Perhaps nightclub fans are already settled on their favorite clubs; but if your club specializes in a particular music type, you can target fans of that genre. Or you could target fans of various alcohol brands or specialty cocktails. Thinking outside the box when it comes to targeting can earn you loyal fans who otherwise might not have thought of your company.

Thou Shalt Not Bore Thy Ad Viewers

Facebook users look at ads all day. The least you can do is give them something worthwhile to look at. If you make a genuinely interesting point in your ad that merits further consideration, people will respect it and be likely to click your ad. There is plenty of good content out there. If you remember Snapple Facts, the one-liners on the bottom of Snapple bottle caps, you have witnessed greatness in the realm of succinct interesting content. A few memorable ones: "Goldfish have an attention span of three seconds." "Animals that lay eggs don't have belly buttons." "Flamingos are pink because they eat shrimp." (I don't know about you, but that last one blew my mind.) Notice Snapple Facts' focus on animals and statistics. Everyone—from kids to senior citizens—is interested in animals. And statistics have a way of neatly packaging information in a palatable way. There is much to be learned here.

Emotionalize Thy Language

Language is powerful, and it is a tenet of advertising to choose language that evokes an emotional reaction in one's audience. In the case of Facebook ads, that means using two or three sentences to sway the viewer to click your ad. If you're really good, the effect you have can go beyond the advertising experience all the way through to a sale. For example, when we ran a campaign on behalf of a private island in the Caribbean, we chose the strategy of encouraging people to stop working so hard and take a vacation. Sentiments such as, "There is no better time than now to take a vacation. Don't you deserve it?" and "Are you working to live...or living to work?" resonated with the audience, making them feel energized not just to click Like, but to book a vacation right away. Although there are many examples of effective messaging (see the next section for a few of them), it is also helpful to break down messages into the individual words that carry the most power. Having a cache of verbal weapons by your side at all times can convert an uninspired ad into your next viral success. To wit, consider the following sentence:

Sleep is precious. Get Kavarian bedding for the ultimate comfort.

Although it may not be obvious, this is an ineffective ad. One just like it got a pitiful click-through rate when it ran on Facebook. And yet, changing a few words around made such a huge impact on the audience that the click-through rate for the ad rose over 500%.

> Cuddling is precious. Kavarian bedding will blanket you with happiness.

Now, I'm not trying to show you that different words have a different effect. I think we all know that. The thinking behind this change is actually much deeper than it looks; it's the result of many months of testing by our Facebook Ads team.

The main words in the first sentence were "sleep," "precious," "bedding," "ultimate," and "comfort." Of those, three out of five are words that we have found to be among the most powerless in the entire language. "Sleep" and "comfort" are words that people have very little emotional associations with (no matter how much they care about both things as actual concepts in real life). "Ultimate" and "precious" have a medium power score, mostly because people see them used frequently enough in advertising copy that they often ignore them. Only "bedding" has a high emotional power score, but mostly because of its connotations as a verb.

In contrast, the main words in the revised sentences are "cuddling," "precious," "bedding," "blanket," and "happiness." Again, bedding has a high emotional power score. But "cuddling," "blanket," and "happiness" have even higher power scores—among the highest in the entire language! Thus, this sentence is packed with resonance for the average Facebook audience member.

If you are interested in learning what the most powerful and least powerful words in Facebook advertising are, see Table 8.1. The words in this table were found by our Facebook ads team to have the most and the least power over Facebook users, as expressed by their desire to click on the ad.

Table 8.1 The Most and Least Powerful Words You Can Use in a Facebook Ad

The Most Powerful		The Least Powerful	
cuddle	joke	museum	seat
ecstasy	blanket	lazy	kerchief
eat	engaged	comfort	failure
proud	valentine	rejected	subdued
diamond	confident	pillow	quiet
easy	diploma	dreary	waste
handsome	excellence	statue	gentle
rollercoaster	sex	bored	prairie
treasure	snuggle	square	table
success	thrill	mantel	tree

Thou Shalt Be Positive

You wouldn't know it from the popularity of the evening news, but many people prefer to follow positive things rather than negative things. In the case of Facebook, it probably has to do with the fact that Facebook uses the term "like" to describe the process of following a page's updates. And so, although you may be *interested* in bad news, you "like" good news. This concept also applies to the way you should phrase a request inside a Facebook ad: always keep your wording positive. We have had far more success asking people to "join the movement" and "help spread the message" than ads that say "this must stop" or "let's bring an end to [something]."

Simplify Thy Language

With all the clutter that exists in our modern-day lives, we have very little tolerance for complexity. This statement is especially true in the case of advertising, which almost nobody wants to look at. The thought in users' minds is, "I'm doing some company a favor by looking at this ad. If it's not easy to understand, I'm outta here." For that reason, you get only one shot to convey a message. If someone has to read your ad twice to understand it, you've lost your potential customer.

Thou Shalt Not Covet Sexy Pictures

It is incredibly tempting to use photos that have a high shock value in your ads, because they actually do lead to more clicks. The problem is, you are not just looking for clicks—you are looking for clicks that come from real interest in what you're selling. If people click on a bikini picture and are sent to a jewelry page, they will almost definitely leave as soon as they realize that a portfolio of additional bikini photos does not await them. By the same token, if you post a picture that is so odd or extreme that people can't help but to click it, you've earned only momentary interest, not purchasing intention. This concept also applies to photos that are violent, funny, or misleading. Keep it on topic!

Thou Shalt Test Thy Ads in Different Demographics

Have you ever heard someone mention a demographic such as "18–35-year-old men" and thought about how different the two ends of that spectrum are? Men who are 18 are contemplating college tuition; 35-year-old men are contemplating college tuition for their kids. Because life is so different in each age and gender micro bracket, it is important to run different ads for each one. Testing for each demographic allows you to see important differences in various groups. This process not only gets you more targeted fans, it helps you understand the highly specific niches that make up your real audience.

Reward Thy Fans

Everyone likes a reward, especially for something as simple as clicking Like or landing on a web page. There is probably something you can give away that doesn't cost you very much. Think in the realm of a download. Maybe an exclusive image, whitepaper, or ring tone. Or think in the realm of a coupon. Obtaining a customer at 10% off your usual prices is better than obtaining no customer at all. Free one-month memberships could also be a great giveaway because they might be a part of your marketing strategy anyhow. By the way, I am not necessarily saying that the item you give away to fans should be low value. Facebook fans are virtual versions of people, and if you treat them well, you may get virtual reciprocation in the form of purchases.

Good Ads and Bad Ads

For most of us, it is more helpful to see examples than to read a list of rules. The following are a number of ads, both good and bad, along with the specific reasons why they succeeded or failed.

Good Ads

The following are some examples of ads that succeeded.

The Intriguing Fish

Figure 8.4 *A successful Facebook ad for a resort in the Virgin Islands. Portions of this image have been intentionally blurred.*

Why It Succeeded—This ad is meant to make a particular resort in the Virgin Islands appeal to scuba divers. As such, it is targeted only to people who like scuba diving. Unquestionably, this picture and its accompanying wording gets the attention of its target group. If the same ad had a picture of a beautiful palm tree, it would be far less effective. (However, if you've got a really great palm tree picture, you could change the target group to palm tree lovers and tailor the text of the ad to that group. Even so, very few palm tree pictures could catch the eye as much as this weird-looking fish.) It's worth noting that a good picture can sometimes define the target group, rather than the other way around.

The Love Seeker

Island (BVI)

Do you dream of a beach paradise with pristine white sand, great big shells & clear turquoise water? Click Like below & discover ████!

Figure 8.5   *Another successful ad for the same resort. Portions of this image have been intentionally blurred.*

Why It Succeeded—This ad, for the same resort, targets females who like the beach. That may seem surprising because the picture does not clearly feature a beach. However, if you read the third commandment carefully, you shouldn't be surprised to see a wee bit of psychology at work here. We found that women who like the beach find it extremely romantic and think of it as a potentially beautiful spot to get married. And so, the picture addresses the target group perfectly.

 Note

Both the intriguing fish and the love seeker ads depict the best-case scenario of an interest. For scuba divers, it paints the picture of being surrounded by incredible, exotic fish. For beach lovers, it portrays the idea of being in love at the beach. Notice that in each ad, the picture gets the user's initial attention, and the text continues the fantasy that the picture started.

The Tattoo Aficionado

Tattoo Parlor

Body art is way more than skin deep. Click Like below to meet tatto artists who will take your body art as seriously as you do.

Figure 8.6 *A successful Facebook ad for a tattoo parlor.*

Why It Succeeded—The thinking behind this ad is that people who have tattoos feel strong emotional connections with their body art. It is targeted to people who like tattoos, and it gets directly at that emotion, affirming that a tattoo represents something much more powerful than just ink on skin. The image is also sentimental (in case you didn't notice, it says R.I.P. at the top), causing tattoo lovers to identify even more with the significance of tattoos.

The Flag Bearer

Travel Agency

If you dream of Greece come join our great big family of Greece lovers. It's free & we'd love to meet you. Just click "Like" below.

Figure 8.7 *A Facebook ad for a travel agency that performed very well.*

Why It Succeeded—The main reason this picture captures the target group's attention is that it contains a symbol that is well known to people who have a connection to Greece. Anyone who likes Greece, especially if they don't currently live there but wish to go, will probably notice this flag. Flags are among the few nonproprietary images that are recognizable by all people. Using a publicly available image that everyone knows to represent your company gives you the same kind of advantage as a large corporation with a recognizable logo. Because most images on the Internet are owned by companies or individuals and thus are unusable in ads, the ones that are free to use are quite valuable—especially if they carry sentimental value.

Man's Best Friend

Adopt a Pitbull

This pitbull would give her own life to save yours if ever she had an oppurtunity. Click Like to meet her & find out if she's your dog!

Figure 8.8 *A highly effective Facebook ad for a canine adoption agency.*

Why It Succeeded—The subject matter of this ad is an animal that is truly beloved by its target group, pit bull owners. To know why pit bull ads are the most successful of any dog ads on Facebook, you'd need to understand that pit bulls are restricted in many cities and local counties around the world, and that there is fierce debate about whether breed-specific bans on these dogs are fair. People who don't own pit bulls are often afraid of them because of the breed's violent reputation. However, people who own pit bulls tend to see them as good-natured, misunderstood dogs, which is why a picture of a sympathetic-looking pit bull arouses such feeling in them. The picture does its job, but it is really the text that makes pit bull owners nod their heads in agreement: indeed, these dogs are as loyal as they come. This is one of the most successful ads we've ever run.

Bad Ads

The following are some examples of ads that failed.

The Skin Shot

Ticket Broker

Get the best seats to the hottest sold-out music & theater performances. Instant availability! Click here and make your night count!

Figure 8.9 *A Facebook ad that got a lot of attention, but ultimately failed to generate sales. These types of ads are seldom accepted by Facebook, anyway.*

Why It Failed—Yes, it got a lot of clicks, but people were clicking for only one reason, and it wasn't for what the company was selling.

The Laugh Riot

Ticket Broker

Feel like everybody is always dumping on you? Click Like below to take master sales training and go from worst to first in 3 months.

Figure 8.10 *Another Facebook ad that seemed to perform well, but generated almost no sales for the client.*

Why It Failed—Just like the skin shot ad, this ad is bound to get clicks—or at least attention—while ignoring the reason why people write ads in the first place: to make sales. The only way this image could work is if it were on a t-shirt for sale. (Although seriously, would *you* wear it?)

The Invisible Image

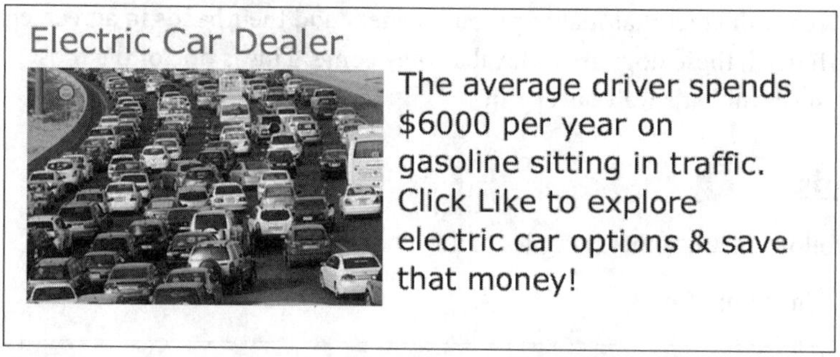

Electric Car Dealer

The average driver spends $6000 per year on gasoline sitting in traffic. Click Like to explore electric car options & save that money!

Figure 8.11 *A Facebook ad that got an exceptionally low click-through rate.*

Why It Failed—People can't even see pictures like this. Constant advertising has numbed our brains so much that we filter out anything as mundane as a row of stopped cars on the highway. That is why it is so important to choose an eye-catching image. And yet, it is not always easy to know what will get people's attention, because many images that seem exciting at first are overused. For example, picture a little boy making a silly face, a fancy car, or a big slice of chocolate cake. We see things like this in daily life or in other ads all the time, and so they are not as powerful as they seem. One picture-finding technique that I like is to quickly scroll through a database of photos and see which ones jump out at you. The image that appeals to you on a more subconscious level has a better chance of being effective inside an ad.

The Plain Jane

Figure 8.12 *A Facebook ad that was too ordinary to capture people's attention.*

Why It Failed—This ad is too general. It is boring. There is no compelling reason to click it.

No Call to Action

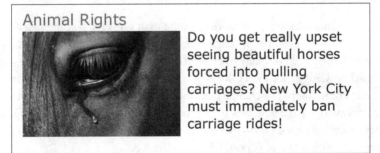

Figure 8.13 *A Facebook ad that does everything right except including a call to action. For this reason, the ad performed poorly.*

Why It Failed—This ad would actually be pretty good if not for the fact that it does not call the user to action. Forgetting to put a call to action in the ad is very common. If there is no request in the ad, people feel far less motivated to do anything.

Converting Facebook Likes into Purchases

Running a successful Facebook ad campaign, while fun, is only a means to an end. As I've reminded you a few times in this chapter, your eye should always be on the prize: purchases. It amazes me how few brands never even ask prior to a campaign's start whether the Facebook advertising they're buying will convert to business for them. There is this notion that having a lot of likes on your page will somehow just "be good for business." Such thinking is lazy and tends to result in a lot of head scratching when campaigns fail to generate sales.

What will bring revenue to your company is consistent testing to see which ads translate to business. As with any form of marketing, if you run your Facebook campaign intelligently, following best practices, you can see within a few weeks whether that channel will be a successful one for your company. After you prove that Facebook can convert even a small number of its audience members into your customers, it's time to start figuring out how to get the most benefit for your dollar.

One of the first things every Facebook marketer should know is that landing tabs (aka "reveal pages") are crucial to customer conversion. You already learned how important these pages are to fan conversion in Chapter 2, but they are even more important to the art of transitioning people from fans to customers. Figures 8.14 and 8.15 contain examples of effective pre-Like landing tabs.

Post-like landing tabs are even more essential than pre-Like landing tabs for converting customers. If people click Like on your page and are then sent right to your wall, they are not likely to convert. If, on the other hand, they are immediately acknowledged for liking the page and given some further ways to interact with your brand, there is a chance their momentum may extend into a purchase. The best way to engage new fans is by showing them a second landing page the moment after they click Like—in a sense, welcoming them into the fold. I refer to this second landing tab as a "post-Like" landing tab.

Figure 8.14 *A pre-Like landing tab. People who arrive on a Facebook page that they don't already "like" through an ad might see this type of tab. Notice the clear call to action, asking the user to Like the page.*

Figure 8.15 *A pre-Like landing tab that contains multiple calls to action. Using multiple calls to action on a pre-Like landing tab will result in far fewer likes to the page, but may ultimately find you your best fans.*

Figure 8.16 *A post-Like landing tab. People who click Like on the tab shown in Figure 8.14 could be directed to this tab rather than being sent to the wall.*

Creating any kind of landing tab requires you to either have a web designer work on it, or use an out-of-the-box landing tab creator. If you want to have a landing tab that has the exact feel of your brand, it is best to use a web designer, just as you would for your website; however, many applications enable you to create a custom landing tab for free, without any coding knowledge. To find some, Google "facebook landing page" and browse through both the paid and organic results.

The main strategic difference between the pre-Like landing tab and the post-Like landing tab is that the pre-Like landing tab typically exists to convince a user to click Like, whereas the post-Like landing tab always attempts to get the user to interact with the brand in some way. A post-Like landing tab could encourage fans to download an e-book or whitepaper, submit an email address to a mailing list, or watch a video.

However, there are exceptions to this rule, as in Figure 8.15, where multiple calls to action are used in a pre-Like landing tab. If you do choose to ask users who have not committed to liking your page to watch a video or submit information about themselves, you risk overwhelming them with requests and losing them as a fan. But those with a single-minded focus on short-term conversions might prefer to know who is ready to act right away, throwing away anyone that might take a few months to convert to a purchaser or subscriber.

Those with a longer-term strategy will rely on building up a base of targeted fans and earning their conversion over a few months. Conversions are earned by updating your page's status consistently and actively communicating with your fan base. This method is, to me, the best overall strategy for capitalizing on Facebook's massive user base. However, it requires a great amount of skill in mass online communication.

I'm ashamed to admit that in college, I thought communications majors were slackers. The ones I knew had text books that examined the art of talking to other people, spent their class time discussing pop psychology concepts, and did group projects around cool advertising campaigns. But now I realize that communicating effectively makes all the difference when it comes time to make a sale online. For most companies, the product doesn't sell itself (ice cream truck drivers, this doesn't apply to you); you have to earn the sale by massaging the relationship.

Communicating effectively on social media takes dedication to good content, a knack for forging relationships with users, and the freedom to act like talking to people on Facebook is your job. Of course, Fortune 500s are pretty much the only ones that can afford to have a dedicated social media communicator who can focus on relationships with fans rather than wearing every hat in the social media department. Even with a limited budget, though, you should be able to outsource targeted social media fan growth while hiring someone to communicate with fans and other social connections. The difference between this position and the more typical "social media guy" (or worse, the "social media intern") is that this person would be first and foremost a communicator, and only secondarily a blog writer, business developer, or what have you. The emphasis in on communication.

When searching for a communicator, know that you are, in effect, searching for a salesperson. Anyone who has ever sought out a salesperson knows how difficult it is to find one—because the small group of people who are truly effective at sales are naturals at it; they were essentially born that way. It is the same with online communicators. The best online communicator that ever worked at my company was hired by chance. She had no experience in social media—in fact, she barely even used Facebook—but she made me laugh at the job interview, and I detected something in her that I thought might translate well online. I later learned that she moonlighted as a comedian, and it all started to make sense. She knew how to appeal to the funny bone of the masses. Though I couldn't quite explain why her writing style was so entertaining to read, it had that special something that made most people I showed it to laugh out loud.

Getting attention to your brand on social media is 80% of the battle. Earning that attention is the communicator's job. The other 20% is offering a compelling reason why your product is worth buying. If you really believe in what you're selling, that other 20% is probably already present.

Using Status Updates to Engage Fans and Convert Customers

In Chapter 6, "Converting Social Search into Profits," I covered all the basics you need to know to use social media properly in a business context. This section applies specifically to Facebook.

When writing status updates on Facebook for the purpose of creating new customers, one rule is key: it's not about you. "But isn't the purpose of a status update to tell people what my company is doing right now?" you might ask. Yes, that is the literal interpretation, the remnant of a sloppy translation of personal profiles to company pages on Facebook's part. If it was more precise, Facebook would call status updates for business pages "fan messages" or something else that conveys that it's all about procuring a certain action, rather than just chatting for the sake of feeling listened to.

Here is what you need to know to use status updates properly for your business:

- **Understand your context**—Facebook is a website where people go to catch up with people and check out photos of friends. It is a place for recreation that has nothing to do with business. Any and all status updates that concern business are an interruption in their experience, which they are sure to find grating. If this were Google, where people often look for things that they can buy immediately, it would not be so offensive to advertise. However, on Facebook, if you are going to advertise you have to do it by building a relationship with fans first and then slipping advertising in casually. Most of the following points cover the relationship-building aspect that will allow your sales pitches to be seen.

- **Be interesting**—If you can be interesting while talking about your industry, that's optimal; however, it is better to say something interesting about *anything at all* than to say something boring about your business. It's highly unlikely that your company is so fascinating to the public at large that it warrants constant status updates. So keep promotional updates to a minimum. Remember that entertaining people on Facebook means saying something gossip worthy. If nobody would talk about it with their friends at lunch, it's not all that entertaining. Good gossip is timely and usually concerns something the reader and their friends would be familiar with. However, the general theme of your status updates should ultimately relate to your business so that your fans think about your company for the right reasons.

- **Use multimedia**—People love pictures and videos. Include them whenever possible in your status updates. Crisp, high-quality images are better received than blurry ones, but it is truly the content that matters. Not only will you get more interaction on your status updates if you use multimedia, but they will be seen by more people, too. Facebook gives a boost in EdgeRank to posts that contain a picture or video.

- **Adopt related causes**—If possible, consider adopting a specific cause your target demographic is passionate about and integrating it into your business. One of the most successful Facebook campaigns we ever did was for a shipping company. After I read a story about dogs dying while being shipped, we proposed adopting the cause of ethical shipping of animals to our client. The company committed to the highest standards for shipping animals and our campaign message—the subject of many of our status updates—became "Animals are NOT cargo! Make us your primary shipping company and show all others that good ethics is good business." The concept of supporting organizations that do the right thing is very powerful. If you use this strategy, remember that the cause needs to be intimately linked to your business. If the same shipping company had given $1 to the ASPCA with each sale instead of taking up ethical animal shipping as its cause, it would not have been as effective.

- **Keep your fans involved**—Facebook is interactive. You should ask fans to comment on the statements you make, questions you ask, or multimedia you share. This is similar to the call to action that you would include in a Facebook ad. Interactivity can also be achieved by running petitions or posting polls. Another interesting tactic is, when you post something important, ask your fans to replicate your message in their own status update. This works best if you are talking about something cause related. For example, an organic clothing company might write: "Fur coats are wrong. Animals don't have to die to keep us warm. Will you contribute your status to passing along this important message?"

After you have built a good relationship with your fans over the medium term—typically, a few months—you should be actively looking to convert your fans into customers. If you've done the relationship-building part correctly, there will be a real sense of trust between you and your fans. A brand people trust will have the "social capital" to post something about its business that has the feel of a sales pitch, as long as it's earnest. For example, a car dealership that regularly communicates in an authentic way with its fans and has attached itself to a clean-air cause might send a status update like this:

> Our company is proud to have supported clean-air auto laws for more than three years. If you are with us in creating a sustainable driving future, come to our event on August 5 where the newest hybrid and electric cars will be on sale.

The sales pitches that convert fans to customers are the ones that don't feel like sales pitches, but rather like genuine requests for people's attention earned through real relationship building. As I mentioned earlier, creating this kind of situation is not for everyone. But now that you know that it is necessary for making sales through Facebook, you can find the right person to undertake the task—or, perhaps decide that Facebook isn't the best use of your marketing time. Above all, I hope that you finally understand what you're getting into when you use Facebook as a marketing tool, and that you now have a clear guide to help you excel at it.

9

Outsmarting
Everything Else

Maybe it's the budding Jewish dad in me, but I can't let you close this book until you know everything you need to know to truly succeed in today's online environment. So far, we've covered Facebook and Google heavily, with a sprinkling of Twitter. The reason I've chosen to focus on these companies is that I believe they will have the largest impact on the marketing you do in the coming five years. However, YouTube and LinkedIn can be extremely valuable to you as well, as can some in-person techniques that go hand-in-hand with the subject matter of this book. In this chapter, I will tell you most of what you need to succeed on those channels.

Attracting Attention on YouTube

Although YouTube is one of the giants of social media, it has not warranted its own chapter because it is much more a capturer of attention than a driver of sales. YouTube visitors are even less in the mood to make a purchase than Facebook visitors are. At least when you're socializing online, there's an opportunity to make socially related purchases via games, local deals, and reports of the things your friends are buying. But when you're being entertained, what do you really feel like buying? Popcorn?

A big success on YouTube is akin to getting a 3-minute programming slot on primetime television: a huge audience will be watching, but very few people will take action from it unless they have gotten familiar with your brand through repeated impressions. Now, I doubt anyone reading this book would say "no" if offered a free commercial. And it would be the same if you were guaranteed a viral video. But if you remove your fame goggles for a moment and actually research the viral videos on YouTube, you'll probably find that most of them earned their creators very little money. Even some of the most viral videos on YouTube, which have more than 100 million views, reportedly generated only a few tens of thousands of dollars.

In fact, the folks who make the most money through YouTube are also spending the most money to produce high quality, consistent content. The most popular YouTube videos are almost all music videos by A-list artists. Those videos required amounts of money that only a big company could supply. The top videos without big budgets are mostly homemade one-offs with no tie to a product or service: a baby laughing, a panda sneezing, a child singing.

But there is a crack of light between the corporations and profitless amateurs. I have seen plenty of content creators become well-known through YouTube and earn a serious amount of revenue without spending much money at all. Before I go into that, though, I'd like to clarify what type of companies *should* be looking into YouTube as marketing channel. That is, who should invest time, energy, and money into YouTube instead of Google or Facebook?

For the most part, YouTube is a place for entertainers. Singers, dancers, screen actors, and comedians can establish their careers or grow them tremendously through the site. Probably the most prominent example of an unknown rising to wealth and superstardom because of his YouTube videos is Justin Bieber. (I promise this is the final Bieber reference of this book.)

A second group that can profit from YouTube consists of those with extremely fun or interesting products. If you were marketing a jetpack, for instance, YouTube would be *the* place to do it. A couple of views of someone lifting off the ground Jetsons-style and the orders would start rolling in.

Another group that is right for YouTube is composed of companies that have such clever ad campaigns that even the highly jaded YouTube audience is willing to look past the advertising and enjoy the content. I have seen many people try and fail at this method, attempting to become the next Old Spice guy. Still, others prosper. One company that stands out as a huge success is Blendtec, whose "Will It Blend?" campaign is a favorite on YouTube. Blenders aren't that interesting, but when you're blending household items such as iPods and golf balls, suddenly people sit up and take notice. The campaign has done well for Blendtec.

A final profitable scenario—and probably the most applicable to readers of this book—is the idea of building thought leadership by recording videos that answer common questions within a niche. Doctors are the perfect example here. A doctor could field common health-related inquiries by video, such as "how to prevent balding" and "how to tell if a mole is cancerous," picking up traffic from the many searches performed each month about these topics. The videos wouldn't require any significant investment, nor would they necessitate much cleverness on the production front. And yet they could result in a huge amount of revenue.

If any of these scenarios can be applied to your business, I hope you give them a try. If not, feel free to skip ahead to the next section.

We'll focus now on strategy. How does one implement a profitable YouTube campaign? The answer is similar to what I've said many times in this book: Create something that is interesting or valuable, tell people about it, and the audience will come. On YouTube, as with all the other social sites, producing content consistently is key. As famous as YouTube is for housing one-hit wonders, its most successful users have hundreds of videos and grow their audiences over the long term.

Those of you who have read *Outsmarting Google* are aware of what I consider to be the ultimate strategy in all of marketing: The Nuclear Football. This technique basically entails creating niche content every day—usually articles, but it could easily be images, charts, cartoons, or anything else people like to look at—and sending that content to bloggers and press on a regular basis. As simple as this method sounds, it is a virtual guarantee to attract traffic through search engines and social media.

On YouTube, Nuclear Footballs are also possible, but in video form. I have coached countless new artists on how to turn their YouTube strategy nuclear, and I will tell you what I tell them: If you produce videos like it's your job, accepting nothing less than excellence, the views will come raining down. What happens after you get the views depends on how you've crafted the video, but you will certainly see the views as long as you put in the work.

To demonstrate an effective YouTube Nuclear Football, I'd like to expand upon the previous example of a doctor who creates videos to answer popular medical questions. Let's make this doctor more real and say that he's a physician who practices in New York City, and his name is Dr. Womack.

If I were in charge of this physician's social media campaign, one of the first areas I would invest in (along with SEO) is a video campaign on YouTube. I would begin by looking up the most common ailments that people search for, choosing 30–40 search phrases and emailing them to Dr. Womack. To research these common ailment searches, I would use a number of sources, including Twitter's real-time search, Google search suggestions, and the Google AdWords Keyword Suggestion Tool. Figure 9.1 shows a query I would try on the Keyword Suggestion Tool:

Figure 9.1   *A search for "how to cure" on the Google AdWords Keyword Suggestion Tool yields some of the most common ailments people look up online.*

As you can see, typing in "how to cure" brought up a list of suggested search terms around how to cure various ailments, from sore throats to pinkeye to a hangover. These are some of the most common medical problems people are looking to cure.

Giving Dr. Womack a week or so to think about how he would address each ailment, I would schedule a time for him to come down to the studio of a trusted videographer. I'd ask that he be available for 3 or 4 hours of filming. On the day of the shoot, the doctor would show up in his white lab coat looking very much the professional. We'd sit him down, get him ready, and then ask him each question exactly as people search for it, allowing him to respond as if he were talking to a patient. His answers would probably take him a few minutes each. By the time we finished recording the responses to 40 inquiries, leaving time for muck-ups and breaks, we'd have 5 months' worth of videos.

Next comes editing. Our editor would be looking to chop each video to 2–3 minutes max, removing any long pauses or hiccups. Each video would start out with a screen displaying the inquiry the doctor is responding to and would end with a photo of the doctor along with his website. If there is budget for it, the editor might even add some still images to the videos to illustrate the doctor's points better.

We'd plan to release two videos per week for 20 weeks. With each video upload, I'd be careful to title the video exactly the same as the phrase people search for when they are researching the ailment—for example, "How to Cure Pink Eye." (Note that the ailment is actually spelled "pinkeye," but because people don't search for it that way, we used the alternate spelling in the title.) I would also tag the video with every keyword I could think of related to the video, such as "cure," "pink eye" "how to" "doctor" "interview" "medical" and "help." I would probably go back to the Keyword Suggestion Tool and see what other words people enter in conjunction with "pink eye" so that I could include those related terms in my list of keywords. When the video was finalized and up on YouTube, it would look something like what's shown in Figure 9.2.

Figure 9.2   *This is how a video might look that was created as part of a YouTube campaign for a doctor.*

After a few weeks, a small library of videos would begin to amass, and slowly, traffic would flow in from people researching their ailments. If the videos are genuinely helpful, users will comment and ask the doctor questions. It is important that someone respond, cautioning that medical advice cannot be given without the doctor and patient meeting in person. Although most viewers will take the free information and run with it, some will feel a rapport with the doctor and contact him for an appointment. In time, a few new patients will turn into dozens. That is how some simple research, a few hours of filming, and little bit of editing can turn into a steady new stream of revenue for a doctor.

Although most video strategies rely on that "x factor" that causes people to become excited by a video, the YouTube Nuclear Football strategy relies on consistency, quality, and quantity. You've got to release at least one video each week. That video must be worth people's time to watch, and there must be a lot more videos they can watch after they've gotten interested. Ultimately, this work will lead to a healthy base of subscribers. When you have a few thousand subscribers, you have a true audience that is waiting to watch whatever you create. And, for those looking to build their brand, there can be no better way to build a personal connection with people.

Using LinkedIn for Business Development

LinkedIn is the ideal tool for business development. If used properly, it can be a map of all the people you know in the business world—and a route to all the important people you don't know. For the few who do not have a LinkedIn account, it is basically a business social network where "connections" are the equivalent of "friendships" on Facebook. There is virtually no personal interaction on LinkedIn; everybody has a business hat on. The goal of using the service is to meet new people who can further your business.

In my experience, there are two types of LinkedIn users: hoarders and quality users. Hoarders accept every connection they are offered, and quality users accept only people that they have a real relationship with.

Hoarders operate on the philosophy that the more people you know, the more business you can do. Anyone that does a lot of "cold" outreach, such as an insurance salesperson or a recruiter, would probably be thinking this way and trying to acquire as many connections as possible.

For everyone else, I recommend the quality user approach. Ed Bogen, a colleague who is one of the most effective LinkedIn users I know, puts it this way: "You should not connect on LinkedIn to anyone who will not call you back within 24 hours."

Ed, who has owned a networking business for 10 years, could easily have thousands of connections. But instead, he has 431. The reason? He personally knows every single one of them.

According to Ed (and my own experience corroborates this), the optimal way to use LinkedIn is by logging in each day for a few minutes to see who your connections have recently connected with. Because the connection is recent, it is more likely that there is fresh energy in the relationship, and it would be possible for you to get an introduction. If you ask for a relevant introduction or two every day, your business could grow untold amounts. We all know that one person can be the genesis of a huge amount of business, and you never know when a person like that is about to come along.

Let's go through a LinkedIn introduction scenario—the kind you could be engaging in every day:

After lunch one afternoon, you are checking your personalized stream on LinkedIn and notice that a friend, Sue, from college just connected with someone who would be an excellent client for your company. Feeling solid about your own reputation in the eyes of this friend, you send her an email (you can request an intro through LinkedIn or simply do it by email; I prefer the latter). Your email goes something like this:

> Hey Sue!
>
> I hope you've been well. I noticed you just connected with Brian Gallagher—how do you know him? I was checking out his background and the company he works for would be a perfect fit for my business. Would you be kind enough to make an intro? Thanks in advance for any help you can provide!

If your relationship with Sue is indeed strong enough, you will receive an email back shortly agreeing to make the intro. At that point it is up to you to make the sale.

Speaking of making the sale, it is interesting to note that this process requires three different "sales." The first is between yourself and Sue: Does she find you reputable enough to risk some of her social capital by introducing you? The second sale is between Sue and the contact. Does this person regard her highly enough to accept an intro from her? The third sale is between you and the contact: Are they ultimately interested in whatever it is that you are proposing to them?

Because so much trust is involved in each of these three transactions, the quality user, in contrast to the hoarder, would be in far better shape to succeed.

Using LinkedIn as a tool for viewing and leveraging business connections is the simplest way to utilize most of its value. After all, at the end of the day, there is no form of marketing more powerful than a personal introduction.

Speaking to Success

If introductions are the most powerful form of marketing, in-person gatherings are the ultimate generators of that power. In an age where social media gets so much air time, it's easy to forget that many businesses make most of their revenues from interactions that take place outside the virtual realm.

The revenue breakdown of my own company, shown in Figure 9.3, is the perfect example of the importance of in-person marketing. More than 25% of our revenue comes from sources that have nothing to do with the Internet.

First Page Sage Revenue Sources

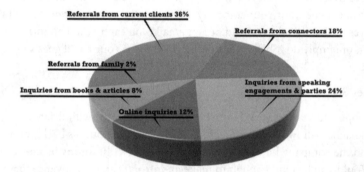

Figure 9.3   *A revenue breakdown of my online marketing company, First Page Sage. Approximately one quarter of our revenue is generated from interactions that began offline.*

Whether or not you are a social butterfly, there is a place for in-person marketing in your company. The best of all in-person marketing scenarios is public speaking, because it puts you into a position of authority and highlights what you do for a living. For those of you who are brave enough to embark upon a career of public speaking, or at least engage in it from time to time, the following sections provide the steps from my own personal experience.

Build Your Bio

To be accepted at even the smallest speaking event, you need to have a bio that positions you as an expert on some topic. Chances are, you are an expert at whatever you have chosen for your career. You will want to compile your experience and accolades into one or two succinct paragraphs that paint you in the most favorable light. While a little bit of spin is okay, accuracy is important because you may be called to task about something you wrote in your bio. It should be easy for you to field questions about your bio, not an exercise in fast-talking.

To illustrate the best practices for creating a successful bio, let's take an average small business owner and figure out the best way to portray him. Our small business owner—let's call him Brent Cardell—is 34 years old and owns a three-person business consulting firm. He got his degree in Business Management from Binghamton University. After college, he worked at a pharmaceutical company for three years in a department that helped to weigh research costs against the benefits of conducting the studies. After that, he drifted for a year or two, offering freelance consulting to family members and entrepreneurial friends, advising them on how to run their businesses more efficiently. He then took a gig at Accenture, a management consulting and technology services company. At Accenture, he was part of a team that advised in the merger of two large tech companies over a 2-year period. Finally, he left the company to go out on his own and start a consulting business. For the next 6 years, he ran BC Consulting through stretches of thin clientele up to today's point, where he has 15 active clients, has brought on two junior consultants to assist him, and makes a good living.

Here is one way his bio could look:

> Brent Cardell has been a business consultant for the past six years. He was previously at Accenture, where he was part of a team that advised on a large tech merger. He also has experience performing cost-benefit analyses for the pharmaceutical industry. He received his degree in Business Management from Binghamton University.

This bio is quite boring. One has to give it to him for honesty, but unfortunately, it would not book him many speaking gigs. A better way of depicting him would be:

> Brent Cardell is an expert in business efficiency. With more than 12 years of experience helping companies to keep a greater share of their revenues, he is frequently tapped to solve difficult challenges related to scaling businesses, increasing profitability, and properly incentivizing management. Having advised on one of the largest mergers in the technology sector, performed high-level analyses in the pharmaceutical industry, and helped to grow numerous small businesses, Brent has valuable experience working with companies of all sizes.

Suddenly Brent has gone from boring to bookable. I began by giving him a niche. He isn't just a "business consultant" anymore; he's an expert at business efficiency. That is a lot more interesting, especially to speaking coordinators. I also got more specific about his areas of expertise, stating that he is "frequently tapped to solve" these "difficult challenges." That is just a fancy way of saying that people ask his advice, but it sounds so much better, like he's an elite force that has been chosen to serve. Finally, I omitted his schooling. Binghamton, although a good school, isn't a big name. Adding his schooling does not help his bio and could possibly hurt him by making him seem like a recent college graduate. I also extended his experience back to the beginning of his career, because he was practicing the same skills before he was in the actual business of consulting.

In general, the thing to keep in mind for a bio is to emphasize your strengths using exciting language. And in the course of your career, create opportunities for yourself that build your bio, such as guest authoring articles for prestigious journals or hiring a publicist to get you some press. The latter might allow you to end your bio with "has been featured in *The New York Times*" or something similarly impressive. It's all about perception. But your bio will only get you in the door.

Speak Anywhere You Can

After you have established that you have something to offer an audience, it's time to do the deed. But before you can start wooing packed rooms, you need to gain some experience. No matter how natural a speaker you are, there are things you'll need to get out of your system that are best done in front of a smaller crowd.

When I first started speaking, I felt uncomfortable working a clicker (the little remote control that moves through your slides). I kept thinking that it would malfunction, or that I would click backward when I meant to click forward. I worried about the awkwardness of holding a microphone in one hand and a clicker in the other, and having no hands free to point or gesture. And speaking of microphones, the first time I got "miked up" with a hands-free mic was bewildering to say the least. Out of nowhere, a sound guy was asking me to run a wire down my shirt, causing me to have to untuck and run my hands under my shirt in front of a partially filled room.

In time, these little quirks of speaking become less a nuisance and more a source of pride. And as you become more comfortable with everything that comes with speaking, you also earn the ability to work a room. I'll never forget my first ever public speech, the first two minutes of which I was completely blacked out—speaking all the while, mind you, but blacked out nonetheless. After about a dozen speaking engagements, I started to get excited before addressing a room, and even though some nerves still remained, there was none of that initial fear.

At the start of your speaking career, you should take any speaking engagement you can get. Some good "starter" audiences are networking groups, business-themed meet-up groups, community gatherings, and adult education sessions at local schools. When you can win over crowds that are fairly forgiving, you're ready to move on to bigger things. (However, I firmly believe that one is never too "big" to speak to a small, local audience, and those kinds of events are often the most gratifying.)

The single most important thing for a new speaker to keep in mind is the value of preparation. If you feel like you know *what* you're talking about and *how* you're going to talk about it, very little else can go wrong. An important caveat to that rule, on the other hand, is never to memorize a speech. A common mistake amateur speakers make is trying to deliver a prepared speech. Few people prefer a prepackaged sermon to a well-organized, genuine release of thought.

Get Friendly with Conference Organizers

As you begin to feel at ease in front of an audience, you will probably start seeking out more and more speaking engagements. After all, speaking *is* addictive: You experience the rush of the room filling up, the pride of passing on valuable knowledge, and the warmth of the applause at the end. But there are gatekeepers to that world, and they're called conference organizers. These folks come in many varieties. Some are stiff and formal; others are party animals. Some are intimidating name-droppers, and still others are quiet observers. One thing they all have in common is that they are constantly being pitched and, at least to some degree, realize the power they have. It is obviously important to build a relationship with them, but you should always do so with a simple integrity. You are you, they are them, and if they dig you, awesome; if they don't, there are plenty more fish in the sea of conferences.

Apply to Many Conferences

You've seen the theme of systematic outreach in this book many times. Those with quality *and* numbers on their side will outcompete those with either quality *or* numbers on their side any day. And so, download a list of conferences in your industry and start looking for the ones you'd like to apply to. The form-filling process is a bit of a pain in the butt, but think of it this way: If it was that easy, everyone would do it. Those long, demanding speaker submission forms act as a filter; don't get caught in it!

After you apply, follow up a lot. Get used to rejection. Know it's their loss, not yours. The unfair part of the speaking world is that even if you submit an excellent application, it may never get looked at simply because some conferences always draw from the same pool of speakers. But you can't easily find out which conferences have this policy, and so you must assume the best and apply away.

Get Creative with Your Presentations

After you land a speaking engagement, it is completely up to you what you do with it. If you choose to just "get through it," the audience will reflect your lack of enthusiasm. If you decide to give a good speech, you will be rewarded appropriately, with a reaction that is generally positive. But if you knock it out of the park, the possibilities become endless. The quality of your presentation correlates to rewards in your career in an exponential pattern. The more you amaze the audience, the greater the possible rewards; but if you perform far above the audience's expectations, there is a chance your speech could change your life.

One of my first speeches was for a small networking group. I didn't realize just how small the group was until I showed up and there were 12 people in attendance. I had prepared a presentation that was meant to move the masses. When I realized how few people were there, I was disappointed, and I resented having to deliver this incredible speech to so few eyes and ears. But I did anyway. The worst part was, there wasn't much reaction afterward, other than one enthusiastic man who told me he loved the speech and was going to call me. Well, to my surprise, that same gentleman was so grateful for the effort I put in that he connected me with several new clients and even introduced me to a speaking coordinator for a prestigious conference. That man became one of the most valuable connectors in my business, and to this day I hold in awe that seemingly pointless speaking engagement I accepted early in my career.

That incident taught me that you always need to bring your best to a presentation because you never know who is watching or what rewards might come from it. Figure 9.4 illustrates this principle.

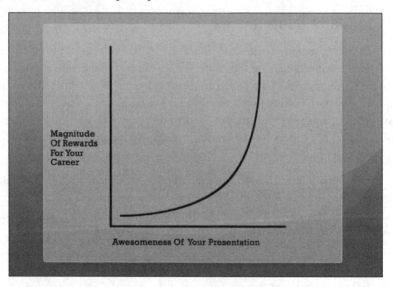

Figure 9.4 *This chart demonstrates the idea that great presentations bring untold rewards to your career.*

To craft a fantastic presentation, think of the time you have with your audience as a blank sheet of paper. Every possibility in the world exists in a blank sheet of paper. You do not need to think in terms of any particular structure, and you certainly don't need to think in terms of PowerPoint. Your presentation can be given without slides; it can be given with a colleague; it can be given with elaborate props; it can be given without speaking; it can involve a megaphone; it can include a live animal; it can get the audience on its feet; it can ask the audience to lie down; it can inform, it can confound, it can surprise; it can be whatever you want it to be.

After a presentation, request feedback. You can either pass around a form or ask the conference organizer for help with recording the audience's reactions. Although feedback can involve criticism, it is very important for you to learn that you can't please everyone.

Videotape your first 10 speeches, and every big speech afterward. A website filled with videos of you speaking will go further than anything else in getting you more speaking engagements.

Above all, call yourself a speaker. If you are out there doing it, then you are one.

Before long, if you truly take pride in serving your audiences, you'll have new speaking engagements all the time.

Managing Your Online Reputation

If you follow the advice in this book, you will soon have a lot of new clients. But with new clients comes new responsibility. In addition to learning how to scale a business, you will need to learn how to deal with your customers in a manner that will help, rather than hurt, your business's reputation.

In my view, there are two types of reputation management: preventative and reactive. It's crucial to practice preventative reputation management every day, and have reactive reputation management in your back pocket should you need it.

Preventative reputation management could also be called good customer service. If you take pride in your business and feel a human connection with your customers, it is unlikely you will have much of a reputation problem. Although in today's online world one nasty review can be very harmful to a business, many companies don't have that issue. What all those companies have in common is a commitment to customer service. No matter how good your product is, somebody is bound to be unhappy with it, but it is how you deal with that unhappy customer that determines the fate of your online reputation. Customer service is so important that I'd wager to say that a company with a phenomenal product but poor customer service would have a much worse reputation than a company with a so-so product but fabulous customer service.

Reactive reputation management is a form of SEO. It involves linking to positive or neutral web pages about your company so that those pages show up higher than any negative results when someone does a search for your company. Typically, a campaign for this kind of reputation management involves creating profiles for your company on all the major social networks. That group of websites can make up the majority of the first page of results for a search of your company's name – and all of them start off with a high degree of Google TrustRank because the pages reside on well-known sites. If you can get a few websites to link to those pages, they are likely to rank above most other results. Registering at least one additional version of your company's name (a .net or .org, for instance) can also help take up space on the first page of search results.

Again, although it's wise to be prepared for the worst, the majority of companies I deal with do not need to use this technique because they focus instead on creating the best possible customer experience. Not only does doing so preserve your business's reputation; it creates referrals, eliminates hassle, and makes coming to work every day a much more pleasant experience for the members of your company.

A Final Word

It is with a heavy heart that I close a full year of researching, interviewing, and writing and send you back to your offices and computer screens—hopefully, a little bit better prepared. As you venture forth in the realm of social media, armed with fresh tactics to outsmart your competitors, I hope you'll bear in mind that success in the Internet age cannot be bought, or won through pure intelligence; it belongs to the scrappy, the dedicated, and the imperturbable, and above all, to the persons who can capitalize on their strengths and recognize their weaknesses.

Finally, the beauty of writing books in the 2010s is that the dialogue is no longer one-way. Indeed, our conversation is far from over—it's simply at a new starting point. See you online!

Index

T

V

W

Y

Z

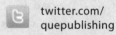
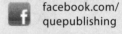
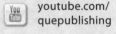

SOCIAL LOCATION MARKETING

Outshining Your Competitors on Foursquare, Gowalla, Yelp & Other Location Sharing Sites

SOCIAL MEDIA ROI

Managing and Measuring Social Media Efforts in Your Organization

OLIVIER BLANCHARD

BLOGGING TO DRIVE BUSINESS

Create and Maintain Valuable Customer Connections

ERIC BUTOW & REBECCA BOLLWITT

FACEBOOK MARKETING

THIRD EDITION

Designing Your Next Marketing Campaign

JUSTIN R. LEVY

que®

Biz-Tech Series

Straightforward Strategies and Tactics for Business Today

The **Que Biz-Tech series** is designed for the legions of executives and marketers out there trying to come to grips with emerging technologies that can make or break their business. These books help the reader know what's important, what isn't, and provide deep inside know-how for entering the brave new world of business technology, covering topics such as mobile marketing, microblogging, and iPhone and iPad app marketing.

- Straightforward strategies and tactics for companies who are either using or will be using a new technology/product or way of thinking/ doing business

- Written by well-known industry experts in their respective fields— and designed to be an open platform for the author to teach a topic in the way he or she believes the audience will learn best

- Covers new technologies that companies must embrace to remain competitive in the marketplace and shows them how to maximize those technologies for profit

- Written with the marketing and business user in mind—these books meld solid technical know-how with corporate-savvy advice for improving the bottom line

Visit **quepublishing.com/biztech** to learn more about the **Que Biz-Tech series**

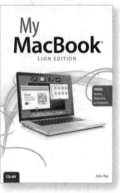

Safari Books Online

Profiting in the Age of Friendship Marketing

EVAN BAILYN

FREE
Online Edition

Your purchase of *Outsmarting Social Media* includes access to a free online edition for 45 days through the **Safari Books Online** subscription service. Nearly every Que book is available online through **Safari Books Online**, along with thousands of books and videos from publishers such as Addison-Wesley Professional, Cisco Press, Exam Cram, IBM Press, O'Reilly Media, Prentice Hall, Sams, and VMware Press.

Safari Books Online is a digital library providing searchable, on-demand access to thousands of technology, digital media, and professional development books and videos from leading publishers. With one monthly or yearly subscription price, you get unlimited access to learning tools and information on topics including mobile app and software development, tips and tricks on using your favorite gadgets, networking, project management, graphic design, and much more.

Activate your FREE Online Edition at
informit.com/safarifree

STEP 1: Enter the coupon code: ZOLKQZG.

STEP 2: New Safari users, complete the brief registration form.
Safari subscribers, just log in.

If you have difficulty registering on Safari or accessing the online edition,
please e-mail customer-service@safaribooksonline.com